The Ties That Bind and Bruise

by

Roger Ball

Roger Ball, PhD | drrogerball@gmail.com

Printed in the United States of America

First Printing, 2019

ISBN 9-781793-397041

Cover design by Kahdijah Venable.

Library of Congress Cataloging-in-Publication Data
Ball, Roger
        The Ties That Bind and Bruise / Roger Ball, PhD
          p. cm.
          Includes bibliographical references.
          1-3CNA5QK

This book is dedicated to my four children Jonathon, Vanessa, Michael and
Addison, my life's partner Senikha Judy-Ann,
and my beloved mother,
Merica Ball

It was the best of times, it was the worst of times, it was the age of wisdom, it was the age of foolishness, it was the epoch of belief, it was the epoch of incredulity, it was the season of Light, it was the season of Darkness, it was the spring of hope, it was the winter of despair, we had everything before us, we had nothing before us, we were all going direct to Heaven, we were all going direct the other way – in short, the period was so far like the present period, that some of its noisiest authorities insisted on its being received, for good or for evil, in the superlative degree of comparison only.

—Charles Dickens

We love because he first loved us.
– 1 John 4:19

How good and pleasant it is when God's people live together in unity
– Psalm 133:1

CONTENTS

PREFACE

I wrote this book because at my core, I am convinced that God is at work in our families and in the world. Additionally, I believe that family is the building block of all gathering spaces where human beings connect. Creating families that are whole is the task of the individual, the couple, the extended family, the faith community, and other social institutions. The goal of this project is to identify the strengths and weaknesses in our families and offer specific guidance as to how we can heal ourselves, each other, and our children. This book is an outgrowth of both my personal and professional work over the last 25 years as a minister, a clinical social worker, public school administrator, college instructor, and, most importantly, as a husband and father.

I am fully aware that, like other bodies of work, this project has its limitations. It does not purport to answer all the questions or challenges faced by families today. However, it is my hope that this book will offer some insights and practical approaches to strengthening and supporting marriage and family life. This is offered through clear recommendations to specific family challenges as well as through the use of scenarios and theological reflections at the end of several chapters.

ACKNOWLEDGEMENTS

This project has been in the making for the last three years and would not have seen its successful completion if it weren't for some very important people.

First, to my best friend and life partner Senikha J. Ball, thank you for always believing in me. Just as importantly, thank you for reading, conducting initial (and final) edits, and providing continuous and critical feedback along the way. Your wisdom and input have only served to strengthen this final publication.

To my friend and colleague Marissa Bailey, thank you for your continued support through my many projects including this one. Thank you for serving as an early reader. Your initial feedback has in some ways shaped the outcome of this body of work. Please know that your input is much appreciated.

To my editor extraordinaire, Jennifer Wyman, thank you for your trusted and rigorous efforts. I am grateful that you have pushed and challenged me to think more inclusively about my ecumenical audience that will be reading this work. Your insight has inspired me to be a better writer, teacher, and preacher. Thank you for journeying with me from my PhD dissertation work to this inaugural book. To say that I could not have done this without you is an understatement. It is said that writing a book is like eating an elephant, and it surely feels that way. Thank you for showing me how to take one bite at a time with finesse and purpose. Your ability to edit and provide feedback with as much passion as this writer is not only exceptional but is also a gift to the profession and the Body of Christ.

Finally, to my faith community, particularly, Family Worship Center and the entire Northeast Region of the Church of God of Prophecy, thank you for the countless opportunities to lead workshops, marriage retreats, family engagement events, leadership development, counseling sessions and sermons on Marriage and Family in an effort to attend to the Ties That Bind and Bruise. Much of this body of work has been inspired by your innumerable stories over these past 25 years of ministry.

THE MYTH OF THE NUCLEAR FAMILY:
LIVING MORE INCLUSIVELY

Call it a clan, call it a network, call it a tribe, call it a family: Whatever you call it, whoever you are, you need one.
—Jane Howard

Like many Jamaican families in the latter part of the 20th century, mine came to the United States in search of opportunity and stability. The first of my family arrived in the 1970s, the last in the early 1990s. My arrival in the summer of 1992 was only made possible by the support of family already living here. Aunt Gee and Uncle Eddie became the stewards of all the newcomers who came searching for a new life. Their apartment building on Paulding Ave. in the Bronx was our touchstone—where we learned how to exist in this new country, and what our new roles required of us. Here is where we learned about surviving in the American workforce, tried new cuisines and different fashions, and endured the blustery New York City winters. The experienced children were tasked with showing those who had recently arrived how to navigate the New York City school system, an educational experience very different from the one we knew.

Without our extended family, integration into a new culture would have been much more difficult. While no one denies that the nuclear family plays a vital role in any community, its function is nevertheless limited. The common belief that the nuclear family is all-sustaining is a restrictive one as it places the family outside of the community. Research confirms that families tend to overcome obstacles better and more quickly when they are supported by multiple generations, diverse resources, and the therapeutic and emotional connections forged within communities.

The African adage, "It takes a village to raise a child" is certainly true, yet it doesn't capture the full scope of intergenerational interdependence. Children not only need both their nuclear and extended families, they themselves are resources that strengthen and bind a family together. Teenagers, for example, can drive grandparents to appointments, take them on a shopping trip, or run errands for them. They can also babysit siblings, help them with their homework, or teach them to ride a bike. Younger children can set the table, take out the garbage, and help with other household chores. No one is denying that raising children requires an enormous amount of resources, but it is unfair to ignore that they too can contribute to the well-being of the family.

The Extended Family: A Potential Economic Benefit

Financial stability and historical shifts in living arrangements[1] have contributed to the isolation of the nuclear family from the extended one.

----

[1] The transient nature of life today has pushed families away from each other geographically and just in terms of how we think about who we live with and for how long.

Naomi Gerstel notes, "The focus on marriage and the nuclear family and the inattention to the extended family distort and reduce the power of social policy" including the construction of the extended family network.[2] More, the rise of same-sex marriage, single-parent homes, divorce, and cohabitation have forced a redefinition of the traditional concept of family. The self-contained, nuclear family that's been the model of the average American home has become unsustainable. It is an unrealistic expectation and, surprisingly, a relatively new one. Throughout most of human history, the family was one of community with multiple generations living together for better or worse.

There is an appreciable economic benefit to low-income families when extended family members live nearby. Middle class nuclear families rely less on their extended family members and are not as likely to reach out to them for financial support during difficult times. If families are isolated from each other geographically, socially, and emotionally, they are at greater risk for poverty and other struggles. However, they will be more inclined to reach out to extended family members if they are within arms-reach.

---

[2] Naomi Gerstel, "Rethinking Families and Community: The Color, Class, and Centrality of Extended Kin Ties," *Sociological Forum* 26, no. 1 (2011), https://doi.org/10.1111/j.1573-7861.2010.01222.x.

The Extended Family: A Potential Reservoir of Emotional Support

I grew up in a relatively large family, at least by today's standards. Being the youngest of six children meant that I was constantly loved and protected. My older siblings watched over me, nurtured me, taught me, and guided me. I belonged. I was an important part of something larger than me. This feeling of belonging extended to aunts and uncles, cousins and grandparents, all of whom helped form and inform my identity.

These family members also stepped in to help raise my siblings and me during a period of my childhood when my mother temporarily moved from Jamaica to Canada in search of work. She then returned to Jamaica for a time, and left again, this time for America, when I was a teenager. During this time I was left in the care of my older sister for about a year.

And, the door swung both ways. I remember a story my mother shared about one of her family members who died during childbirth. My mother, who was nursing one of my brothers, quickly stepped in and offered to nurse the child. This story brings to light another absurdity of the nuclear family. In this country, it is normal and even expected that two adults assume the responsibility of raising two or more children from birth to age 18 (and, in many instances, beyond) without the assistance of anyone besides their family. In fact, members of the community including teachers, counselors, social workers, and the clergy all work in tandem to support the health and wellbeing of both parents and children. Life is uncertain, and a cataclysmic tragedy such as the death of a woman in childbirth can leave the infant's future in the hands of fate. Without the intervention of other individuals, that child would be left vulnerable to the world, which can be very brutal.

Although we are a thousand miles and several decades removed from Jamaica and Guyana (where my wife is from), our connection with our heritage remains strong. We recognize the importance of carrying on our traditions and make sure we instill in our children the conviction that community and family are not mutually exclusive and that remaining together is fundamental to our success and survival.

My wife and I keep our connections with our extended family strong. Although my aunts and uncles now live in Florida—quite a distance from New York—we visit fairly frequently. These trips to Florida are more than just reunions. They keep our family history alive. My Aunt Gee is the family historian. For as long as you're willing to listen, she will regale you with stories about those that came before us, the secrets, the joys, and the surprises of the rich tapestry that is our story. These treasures and nuggets of the past would be forever lost without someone to hear and remember her words and repeat them. Only family understands the importance of keeping them alive. If we lose our story, we lose our identity, another reason why storytelling remains central to both formation and transformation of family. We also make room for connecting with my wife's family within the US and in Guyana.

Many if not most African-Americans cannot find records of their family lines in genealogical histories or online databases. Sold to the highest bidder—much like cattle—our ancestors were shipped off to the United States, Europe, and the Caribbean as nameless cargo unworthy of documentation. Our histories were shared orally, passed down through the years in stories told and retold until they became etched in the tapestry of family memory.

Today, oral tradition remains a prominent medium of record keeping for many African-American families. It is why I sit attentively at my Auntie's feet, committing every story to memory, well aware that I stand in the shoes of those who came before me. I choose to be the guardian of our history; to keep it alive, to continue the oral traditions, to keep the fabric of our family strong by teaching those who come after me just how immutably connected they are to those that came before me.

I recall a time I was preaching at the Church of God of Prophecy in Old Harbor, Jamaica where my family has a long history. Standing at the pulpit on that sweltering Sunday morning, I looked out at the congregation and saw faces that I recognized from my childhood. I saw my father's sister, Aunt Babs, who made sure she sat close to the front to see me preach. When I finished, my aunt threw her arms around me. She exclaimed, "I wish Papa was alive to see this. You sound, move, and preach just like him." These were the words I needed to hear. My eyes welled with tears. I'd never met my grandfather, but what she said made me realize I wasn't preaching out of time or out of tradition. My context is the story, the tradition. I have become a preacher in the order of both of my grandfathers, Charles Levy and Kenneth Ball.

More recently, I was invited to Bermuda to speak about mercy and truth. At the end of my sermon, an elderly lady approached me and asked, "Dr. Ball, is your family from Rechies?" I knew instinctively where this was going. "Yes," I said. Then she said, "Do you know Rev. Kenneth Ball?" I got goosebumps, as I always do whenever anyone makes the connection. I responded proudly, "Yes, I'm his grandson!" I don't know why I feel so connected to him. Maybe it is because he was known as a man of integrity. Maybe it is because I am told he helped anyone in need. Maybe it is because his blood courses through my veins or that he was a preacher. Or, maybe it is because I understand that we are a people whose history has been created by others, shaped and reshaped by others, told and written by others. In order to keep our histories alive, it is imperative that we retain the connections we have by remembering the past and handing it on to future through poetry, song, art, and the stories we tell to our children.

Not only do I try to instill these values in my own children, as a teacher, I invite my students on all sorts of intellectual journeys into their past and future. I often give assignments that require them to reach back into their childhood as well as ones that invite them to imagine their futures. One of my favorites is the genogram project. A genogram is a visual representation of a family tree accompanied by a key that represents changes, transitions and relationship structures within the family system.

This particular assignment forces students to excavate hidden memories, sit with older generations, ask questions, and discover information about their families that they didn't know before. This new information can either evoke feelings of pride about the student's heritage and ancestry, or it can cause a student to become conflicted if revelations of divorce, premature deaths, mental illnesses, or other disturbing facts emerge.

In the following activity, you are invited to construct a simple genogram extending back four generations if possible. (If you can't go back that far, go as far as you can.) A genogram is just one tool that we can use to examine our family history and patterns. Try to have an open mind when doing this activity. Take your time, don't do it all in one day. Write down questions that you do not have the answers to. Reach out to extended family members and older generations for information they might have in their memory banks.

Activity: Constructing Your Genogram

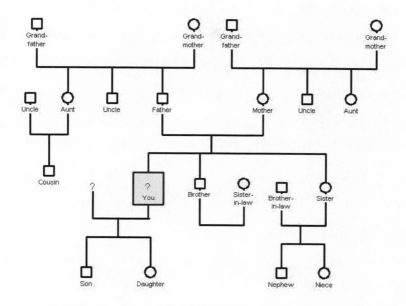

- What patterns emerge about ages of births and deaths?
- What are some patterns on one side of your family that are different from the other?
- What relationship patterns do you see in your family history, and do they persist today?
- How has each generation impacted the other positively and negatively?
- What did you discover about your knowledge about your own history?
- Who did you have to ask for lost information to complete the genogram?
- What traditions have been lost along the way and why?
- How have migration, class, and conflict disrupted relationships?

Finding Your Story in Scripture—Ruth's Sacrifice, Ruth's Reward

The Book of Ruth in the Old Testament is a beautiful example of how family can assume many forms and how the common denominator in all families is love. As you read, consider how a daughter-in-law's loyalty and sacrifice gained for her the bounty of family, love, and security.

> *"For where you go I will go, and where you lodge I will lodge. Your people shall be my people, and your God my God." (Ruth 1:16)*

Strengthening the Ties that Bind	Helpful Resources
"The African adage, "It takes a village to raise a child" is certainly true, yet doesn't capture the full scope of intergenerational interdependence. Children not only need both their nuclear and extended families, they themselves are resources that strengthen and bind a family together."	Ancestry.com The Freedmen's Bureau Project www.discoverfreedmen.org/ LiveWell Intergenerational Resources www.livewellsd.org Generations United www.gu.org Penn State Intergenerational Program aese.psu.edu/extension/intergenerational

II

WHEN FAMILIES DO MORE HARM THAN GOOD

Families living in dysfunction seldom have healthy boundaries. Dysfunctional families have trouble knowing where they stop and others begin.
—*David W. Earle*

Families are defined by their culture just as much as they are by blood, sometimes more so. This being true, we are not only carriers of genes but also of customs and traditions. We pass down communication patterns, rituals, approaches to conflict resolution, and problem solving skills from one generation to the next in much the same way family recipes are handed down. And we do all this without realizing that we may very well be carrying something dysfunctional into the future. We pass on domestic violence norms and call it Biblical—"spare the rod and spoil the child." We pass on gender stereotypes when we hinge a woman's value solely on her ability to have children and perform domestic duties. We tell our sons to "stop crying like girls;" and, when they listen to us, we call them heartless. Thus, men learn that crying is a form of weakness, women and girls cry because they are weak, and the colder and more callous they are the more attractive they become. In the end, we teach boys to curb basic human emotions to the point where they lose the very memory of how to weep.

When we pass on these types of disordered life lessons to our children, we send them to their future selves and future families broken, and in turn, they break their offspring—the cycle in perpetuity. Part of the problem is that when broken people form unions, they are often not willing to put in the work to become whole. I cannot stress enough that we have the power to undo the past not by going back and changing it—as we know, that's impossible—but by intentionally changing the script in the now as it plays out to create a new end.

The Story of Elisa Izquierdo

Dr. Bessel Van Der Kolk, author of *The Body Keeps The Score,* said, "We have learned that trauma is not just an event that took place sometime in the past; it is also the imprint left by that experience on mind, brain and body. This imprint has ongoing consequences for how the human organism manages to survive in the present."[3] Over the years, I have seen and heard many stories about dysfunctional families and the horrors they inflict on each other. I have had to make one too many calls to the NYS Central Registry to report alleged abuse by parents against their own children. The irony is that social workers and child welfare organizations are often made out to be the villains in these situations. Even when intervention is clearly warranted, social workers and other mandated reporters are accused of disrupting families by monitoring parents' behaviors, mandating parenting classes, and in some cases removing children from the home. When cries for help fall on

---

[3] Bessel Van der Kolk, *The Body Keeps the Score,* New York: Viking, 2014, 21.

deaf ears, however, catastrophe often follows. Van Der Kolk compares traumas experienced by soldiers in war zones to the daily suffering inflicted on many children by their family members and its lasting effects of the growing mind. He notes, "for every soldier who serves in a war zone abroad, there are ten children who are endangered in their own home ... . This is particularly tragic since it is very difficult for growing children to recover when the source of terror and pain is not enemy combatants but their own caretakers."

Around my first year of college, a grim story broke in New York City about the death of six-year-old Elisa Izquierdo. Because Elisa was born to crack addicted mother, Awilda Lopez, custody was granted to her biological father, Gustavo Izquierdo. Guz was a loving and caring father, and, for the first few years of her life, Elisa had security, love, and stability. Her mother eventually went to rehab, got clean, and was granted shared custody of Elisa. Unfortunately, Guz developed terminal cancer. After his death, Elisa, having no other options, was at the mercy of a cruel mother and a sadistic stepfather who beat her regularly. Her abuse was well known by her school and neighbors who tried to intervene many times. They were unsuccessful. Their calls to the child protective services were ignored and Elia's abuse continued unchecked. On November 22, 1995, Elisa's torment came to an end when she received a fatal blow by the hand of her mother. *Newsweek* reported:

As rescue workers pulled Elisa Izquierdo from her bed, they found deep-red blotches—welts, cigarette burns—pocking her entire body. On her right side, near the kidney, was an enormous bruise, and she had more bruises on her face and around her temples. There were ghastly wounds around her genitals. The bone of her right-hand pinkie was jutting through the skin. Fireman Michael Brown began CPR, but it was hopeless. "In my 22 years of service," said police Lt. Luis Gonzalez, "this is the worst case of child abuse I have ever seen.[4]

Tragically, Elisa's fate is not uncommon. In the United States, 25% of violent crimes against children are perpetrated by family members.[5] Just because we do not hear about them does not mean that they don't happen. Elisa's story garnered attention because of the gross failure of the child welfare system.

Children under 5 are most at risk of being killed by a family member. Once children go off to school, school personnel are trained to recognize child abuse and will report warning signs as mandated by law. In the case of Elisa, however, reporting did not stop the abuse. Thank goodness, since those days, the child welfare system has improved its responsiveness to allegations of child abuse.

---

[4] Mark Peyser, "The Death of Little Elisa," *Newsweek*, December 10, 1995, https://www.newsweek.com/death-little-elisa-180258.

[5] Michelle Kirby, and Katherine Dwyer, "Violent Crimes Against Children," *OLR Research Report,* September 27, 2013, https://www.cga.ct.gov/2013/rpt/2013-R-0329.htm.

The Predator You Know and Trust

Sexual abuse of minors is often perpetrated not by strangers but by family members, friends, neighbors, babysitters, and other individuals known to the youngster. Too often, non-biological guardians perpetrate physical and sexual violence against the children of their partners. Jesus made his position about children clear. He blessed them and invited them into conversation and fellowship. He also partnered with a young boy to start a canteen that would feed thousands of people in a single day.

> I tell you, once and for all, that unless you start over like children, you're not even going to get a look at the kingdom, let alone get in. Whoever becomes simple and elemental again, like this child, will rank high in God's kingdom. What's more, when you receive the childlike on my account, it's the same as receiving me.
> But if you give them a hard time, bullying or taking advantage of their simple trust, you'll soon wish you hadn't. You'd be better off dropped in the middle of the lake with a millstone around your neck. Doom to the world for giving these God-believing children a hard time! Hard times are inevitable, but you don't have to make it worse—and it's doomsday to you if you do. (Matt 18:2-7)[6]

We can't talk about family values if we are not speaking out against the damage that family members can inflict on one another. From domestic violence to psychological abuse, families are in desperate need of healing. This is where faith communities come in. They can help families break the cycle of the generational curse that we so often talk about. The

---

[6] The Message Bible translation.

pulpit remains one of the key spaces for us to advance a gospel that inspires people to practice a faith that is inclusive of healthy family relationships. One way to do this is through storytelling. Whether it's the story of Cain slaying his brother Abel (Gen 4), or Abraham and Sarah struggling with the reality of infertility (Gen 16), or the rape of Tamar by her half-brother Amnon (2 Sam 13), Biblical stories have the power to open taboo doors giving us access not only to ancient history but also to our own history and current realities. They can help us reimagine our own family structures and rewrite them in a way that's healing.

The Myth of the 'Family Curse'

In my faith community, people use the term "family curse" to describe a spell that has been placed on the family going back generations. At the risk of being too blunt, this is hogwash. No doubt, history repeats itself; but there is no such thing as a magical hex that controls our behavior. The only family curses are the ones we perpetuate when we pass dysfunctional life lessons on to our children. We need to demystify what we mean when we say "family curse" by discovering its inception, noting impacts on our lives, and devising ways to think, feel, and live differently.

Family is the primary institution through which we learn how to exist in the world. By digging into our family histories, we can begin to unravel the underlying source of our learned behaviors, both good and bad. Of course the same is true for how our families are impacted by other social institutions such as churches, schools, neighborhood, peer relationships, and other influencing entities such as social media, politics, and social policies.

When I was a teenager, I worked in a small dry cleaning store just outside of New York City that was owned and operated by my pastor who eventually became my father-in-law. There was a particular customer, a medical doctor, who came in every few weeks. He would bring in a few shirts and what seemed like 80 pairs of pants each time. One day my father-in-law asked him why so many pairs of pants. He said that growing up he did not have enough, so now that he could afford them he bought them in bulk. A deeper conversation with this successful doctor would probably reveal a person that had to wear "hand me downs" as a boy. Growing up poor left such an indelible mark on him that he likely spent his adult years hoarding and spending in excess. He, like so many of us, remained mired in the past, never able to bury the memories of being scorned and mocked because of his clothing.

People develop all sorts of coping mechanisms to combat fear and anxiety, many of them not productive, and some of them harmful. This man used hoarding as a way to cope with the (imagined) threat of poverty. What we've endured in our childhood, whether it's the way we were treated by members of our families or bullying we endured, compels us to develop some form of survival mechanism (however unhealthy) to stave off the fear, anger, and helplessness those memories bring. Even when those threats are long gone, we still function as though they were present. The doctor who came into the dry cleaners had more than enough money to buy whatever he wanted and enough education to make sense of his past. Yet, he remained captive to his obviously disordered compulsions. It is exceedingly difficult to unlearn behaviors when we remain in denial about why they exist. Only when we are able to make connections between our current actions and the past can we learn ways of leveraging those past experiences in such a way that they enrich our lives rather than hold us back, thus enabling us to be healed.

I believe in the power of prayer and that praying with intentionality has enormous benefits. In fact, the research is clear on the positive and miraculous effects of prayer. Dealing with a "family curse" requires prayer that is focused and maintains an awareness of (1) its historical roots, (2) its personal impact, (3) how you react physically and emotionally when triggered by memories of the past, and (4) how to disrupt dysfunctional patterns that have been passed down to you. Some people are able to work through these on their own while others need the help of professional clinicians and pastoral counselors. Still others need the help of faith communities and social and intimate relationships to find healing over time.

First, we need to define the concept of the "family curse" in more accessible terms to demystify it, thus neutralizing its power over our lives. Some terms to replace "family curse" might be:

- Traditioning
- The passing on of values and practices

- Becoming our history
- Intergenerational practices

This kind of language takes the mystery out of the "family curse" and concretizes it into patterns and dysfunctional structures that are then passed down to the next generation. These are the ties that bruise. To further this point, let's consider how the following dysfunctional family dynamics might impact children and adults in the future:

1. Lack of parental affection
2. A depressed mother who walks away from her family
3. An alcoholic father

Lack of Parental Affection

Many children grow up in households where parents provide for their physical well-being but give little thought to their emotional needs. The reasons for this lack of affection can be cultural, social, or the result of learned behaviors over time. In these homes, love is demonstrated not in endearing or affectionate words but in deeds. Parents do not tell their children they love them nor do they inquire about their mental or emotional wellbeing. Denied the basic human need for love and affection, these children grow up insecure and emotionally isolated. In his book, *The Bridge of San Luis Rey*, Thornton Wilder tells the story of five ordinary people traveling in Lima, Peru who perished when the bridge they were on collapsed. This tragedy led a young priest, Br. Juniper, to ask the ageless question of why these five had to die. In his investigation into their lives, he found that they were no better or worse than the millions who escaped death that day. His conclusion was this, "But soon we shall die and all memory of those five will have left the earth, and we ourselves shall be loved for a while and forgotten. But the love will have been enough; all those impulses of love return to the love that made them. Even memory is not necessary for love. There is a land of the living and a land of the dead and the bridge is love, the only survival, the only meaning."[7] Br. Juniper's insight is filled with profound truth. In the end, it's not material resources that give our lives meaning. There are many people in the world that are poor yet fulfilled and many that are rich yet empty. I do understand why some parents feel guilty or inadequate when they cannot afford to give their children things they want. But, children understand much more than they are often given credit for. They will grasp that their parents might not be able to give them everything that they want or need. What they will not understand is why their parents withhold love. Love can't be substituted with material resources because it is not rooted in the material but the immaterial. 1 John 4:8-10 tells us:

> My beloved friends, let us continue to love each other since love comes from God. Everyone who loves is born of God and experiences a relationship with God. The person who refuses

---

[7] Thornton Wilder, *The Bridge of San Luis Rey*, New York: Harper Collins, 2014 (reprint), 107.

to love doesn't know the first thing about God, because God is love—so you can't know him if you don't love. This is how God showed his love for us: God sent his only Son into the world so we might live through him. This is the kind of love we are talking about—not that we once upon a time loved God, but that he loved us and sent his Son as a sacrifice to clear away our sins and the damage they've done to our relationship with God.

Children deprived of their parent's love grow up craving affection at any cost, even seeking it from sources that are dubious and suspicious. They might even know that the object of their affection is not good for them, but will take dangerous risks just to fill the void that was created by the absence of their parents' love and affection. Others grow up behaving exactly the way their parents did. They knowingly or unknowingly reconstruct their own lives as replicas of their parents' while wounding the next generation. They might even wear those practices as badges of honor telling their children, "when we were growing up, we knew that our parents loved us not by what they told us but by what they did. We didn't need to hear them say 'I love you.' They worked hard and provided for us ..." as a means of legitimizing their own approach to parenting. It was C.S Lewis who said, "You can't go back and change the beginning, but you can start where you are and change the ending." We don't have to be victims of the past, and we don't have to agree to be conduits of past destructions. More, we certainly can't change the past. However, we can and should start right where we are and make a valiant effort in creating an ending that is antithetical to our beginning.

So, what can you do to change your personal narrative if you feel like your family did not know how to love you the way you needed to be loved?

1. Commit yourself to fully understanding your family history and understand that your mother's and father's parenting style was never about you as a person. It says nothing about how lovable you are or how deserving you are of love.

2. Learn to love yourself for who you are. Embrace your individuality and your strengths.

3. Try your best not to repeat what was done to you. Love unconditionally. Tell your children and spouse that you love them. If your parents are alive, give them what they might not have been able to give you—affection and love. You might just become their teacher-healer.

4. Don't be too hard on your parents. You might even need to forgive them for their trespasses and ignorance in not loving you the way you needed for them to love you. In the end you might heal both yourself and your parents as well as your own children, three generations in one fell swoop.

A Depressed Mother Who Walks away from Her Family

We cannot control the family we are born into. The children of Prince William did not ask to be born into Britain's royal family. Neither did the child born to the teenage mother and father in Harlem or the child of the young mother living in a hut in the slums of Johannesburg ask for their lot in life. The same is true for 8-year-old Samantha whose 28-year-old mother abandoned her when she was 7. Diagnosed with major depressive disorder when she was pregnant, Samsara spent much of her 20s in deep apathy and listlessness. Her depression stemmed from having her heart broken by a young man. She thought he loved her, but he left when she told him that she was two months pregnant with their baby. He never looked back and she never sought him out. Samantha never met her father and lived with a mother who was never quite available to support her basic needs. Samsara was an inattentive, apathetic mother who was not consistent in taking her medication for her mental illness. This had a definitive impact on Samantha who not only suffered from neglect but had to witness her mother's suffering. Some of Samsara's symptoms according the Diagnostic and Statistical Manual (DSM V) were a depressed mood, diminished interests, feelings of worthlessness or guilt, an inability to concentrate, and indecisiveness.

As her mother spent most days in bed, Samantha learned to get herself up in the morning, get dressed, prepare breakfast, and make her way to school. She saw other parents taking their children to school while her own mother was asleep in bed. She always wanted a mother who was more involved. She often wondered about her father and if maybe he would take her to live with him. On her 7th birthday, her mother bought two tickets from New York to South Carolina, handed her over to her grandmother and left, never looking back. Unwanted by either parent, Samantha's feelings of abandonment run deep. She will struggle with these feelings throughout her life and will need to work hard not allow them to impact her relationships with her partner and her children.

An Alcoholic Father

Most of us have at least one alcoholic in our family. Too many times we see and hear the devastating effects of alcohol use, abuse, and addiction on children and families. The issue of substance abuse includes not just alcohol but also cannabis, prescription drugs, and other narcotics. Substance abuse breeds dysfunction in our families and creates unsafe living conditions for all members of the household. In many instances, children learn from parents that the best way to deal with conflict and difficult times is to turn to the bottle or the medicine cabinet as a way of coping. These are the ties that bruise. More than we may realize, family curses are patterns of learned behaviors that we assimilate through observation and inculcation. There's a story about a young wife who grew up watching her mother cut off the tail of the fish every time she prepared it for the oven. As an adult, she prepared fish the same way. One evening during dinner prep, her daughter asked, "Why do you need to cut off the tail?" to which she replied, "I am not sure. My mom always did it this way." Unsatisfied with the answer, the youngster called her grandmother and asked the same question. Her grandmother answered, "My curious child, that's a great question to which I don't have the answer; but what I can tell you is that growing up my mother did the same thing. I guess it's now a tradition in our family when cooking whole fish." Still undeterred by subpar answers from both her mother and her grandmother, she stopped by her great grandmother's apartment and asked, "Nanna, why do we need to cut off the fish tail before putting in the oven?" Her great grandmother said, "Child, who is still doing that?" "Mom and Gramma do it." "Well," said Nanna, "you see, when I was growing up my mother had a wooden stove that was so small that we had to cut off the tail of the fish, the ends of the pot roast, and anything else that was too big to fit." She continued, "But these are modern times. Your mother and grandmother have state of the art stainless steel stoves so I am sure they don't need to waste the tail of the fish by cutting it off." This story has many versions, but the point remains the same; we are social creatures who bring language, food, music, and culture patterns with us into the future. An alcoholic father who becomes violent with his wife and children will leave them with deep mental and emotional scars. Some of those children will experiment with alcohol, while others will vow to stay away at all costs. Imagine a girl who had to deal with an alcoholic father growing up and all that that would entail. Imagine she grows into woman who falls in love with a man that is an alcoholic. Now, imagine what it would be like for her to relive her childhood trauma and have to contend with similar behaviors in her own intimate relationship. Some would argue that this woman is socialized to fall in love with men that are like her father. These are the ties that bruise.

No family is perfect. And, truly, no family needs to be. Consider this, the depressed mother did not one day say, "I am going to choose to be incapacitated by my depression." Nor did the father decide as a boy to grow up to be an alcoholic. Most parents will tell you that while they might have done the best they could at the time, looking back they wish they had the wisdom, patience, and strength to love their children the way they needed to be loved. The reality is that we don't always have the emotional or psychological resources to meet the needs of our children. Because hope is a cornerstone of our lives, we should move away from the belief that we don't have the wherewithal to support the emotional needs of our children and embrace the notion we might not have the wherewithal – YET. In her ground-breaking work on Fixed Mindset vs. Growth Mindset,[8] Carol Dweck has argued convincingly that we should not pigeonhole ourselves into restrictive, binary categories of "can" or "cannot." We do ourselves a disservice when we say things like, "I can't do math," or "I can't cook." This closes the door before it has even been opened. Rather, we see our potential and reach for "not yet." "I can't play the piano *yet*." We might not be the kind of persons

---

[8] Carol Dweck, *Mindset: The New Psychology of Success*, (New York: Random House, 2006).

we would like to be, but we can work towards being better to and for each other.

The Power of Yet

Some of the most powerful family meetings I have ever facilitated have been between teenagers and their parents. I have seen teens confront parents for sending them away to live with other family members because of homelessness or other complicated situations. I have also seen parents apologize with deep agony in their voices and eyes as they tried to explain that it wasn't meant to be abandonment, that they were looking out for their best interest. I have listened to those children tell stories of how they were mistreated by others in the absence of their mothers and fathers, how they have lost a sense of trust that their parents would always be there. And just as importantly, I have seen families repair those bonds to be even stronger than they were before the separation. If you have some fences to mend, the power of YET is still on your side. If you have some apologies to make, the power of YET is still on your side. If you need to start telling your family that you love them, the power of YET is still on your side.

Reflection: Healing Old Wounds

1. What would it take for you to acknowledge to your family that some decisions that you have made did not serve them well?
2. How might they respond to such an acknowledgement?
3. What might be the potential consequence (good and bad) of such an acknowledgement?
4. Finally, how might you prepare yourself to engage in this conversation?

Paul Lawrence Dunbar's poem Sympathy reminds us that we often beat ourselves against the bars that hold us captive. Sometimes those bars are our family history. Sometimes in order to be free we must engage in difficult and painful conversations so that hopefully, by the grace of God, we emerge better than we were when we entered those conversations.

> *I know why the caged bird beats his wing*
> *Till its blood is red on the cruel bars;*
> *For he must fly back to his perch and cling*
> *When he fain would be on the bough a-swing;*
> *And a pain still throbs in the old, old scars*
> *And they pulse again with a keener sting—*
> *I know why he beats his wing!*

Finding Your Story in Scripture—Sibling Rivalry (Gen 37)

Let's face it, every family has some dysfunction. It's when dysfunction gets out of hand that you have to worry. As parents, we are responsible for the family dynamic by setting good examples, being equitable with our time and attention, and making sure everyone feels safe and loved. Jacob played favorites and the results were disastrous. As you read Joseph's story, consider what Jacob could have done differently to prevent his son from being lost for so long.

Strengthening the Ties that Bind	Helpful Resources
"We cannot control the family we are born into. The children of Prince William did not ask to be born into the royal family. Neither did the child born to the teenage mother and father in Harlem or the child of the young mother living in a hut in the slums of Johannesburg ask for their lot in life."	National Center for Missing and Exploited Children http://www.missingkids.com (800) 843-5678 National Domestic Violence Hotline (800) 799-7233 Samhsa's National Helpline—Helps people locate facilities to treat addiction and mental health issues 800-662-HELP (4357) http//:Findtreatment.samhsa.gov National Alliance on Mental Illness https://www.nami.org/find-support Growth Mindset For Parents https://www.mindsetkit.org/growth-mindset-parents

III

MAKING MARRIAGE WORK

It is not a lack of love, but a lack of friendship that makes unhappy marriages.
—Friedrich Nietzsche

The decision to get married is one of the biggest, happiest, and most expensive ones many of us will ever make. If we do it right, we can find lifelong happiness and meaning; do it wrong, we can spend the rest of our lives paying for it. Marriage is an idea that holds us captive with its endless possibilities and the promise of forming a connection and creating a future with another person. As alluring as it is elusive, for many it remains just that, a dream unrealized. This is especially true for African Americans and other minority groups.

Statistics Do Not Lie

Among my fellow theologians, I find myself swimming against the tide regarding the processes of entering, maintaining and, yes, exiting marriage when it no longer becomes viable. We all agree on the sacredness of marriage and its divine roots. We further agree that marriage is God's gift to us. This concept of marriage as a gift has engendered some questionable beliefs in many church communities. Among them are:

1. Finding a spouse means that you must wait for God to send someone to you.

2. Once you find that person you will know without a doubt that s/he is the one.
3. There's such a thing as a God ordained union that requires little work.
4. Love is only legitimized when found within one's own faith community and sanctioned by members of said community.

Regarding myths one and two, I have long raised questions about the male to female ratio of adult members of our churches. Research done by Pew found that in the US, women are more religious than men. In 2014, 60% of women surveyed said that religion is very important to them while only 47% of men reported feeling the same. The trend was the same when it came to religious practices such as attending weekly church services (40% vs. 32%) and daily prayer (64% vs. 47%).[9] Churches that tell women and men to wait for the Lord to send them someone must understand that this person does not have to be someone from the same church or even the same denomination. Possibly more importantly, churches need to provide spiritual and contemplative instruction to single Christians teaching them how to:

1. Respond to the call of God in their singleness
2. Minister to these members based on where they are

---

[9] Pew Research Center, March 22, 2016, "The Gender Gap in Religion Around the World"

3. Address the challenge that there are just not enough men in our churches[10]

Regarding the third misconception, once two people come together there are plenty of opportunities for conflict. When we are angry with our spouse, most of us don't say, "Let's hold hands and pray." A successful marriage requires constant work. Often, young marriages crash and burn because of false hope and misguided expectations. If you are considering marriage, it's critical that you find a seasoned counselor who will spend time discussing the many areas of marriage—finances, parenting, the in-laws, conflict resolution, and other matters. If folks wait until there is problem to voice their position and expectations, it may be too late.

On the fourth faulty belief, how often have we gotten the sense that our faith community has not taken a welcoming attitude towards someone a congregant is dating? I question the need to police whom anyone chooses to love. We might know little to nothing about other areas of people's lives such as work, interests, pain, family conflicts; however, we spend much time making value judgments about their romantic partners. We all want to be supported and nurtured by our faith communities even if they disagree with our choices.

---

[10] On this last point, we must face the fact that we have not done a good job of attracting, ministering to, and keeping men in our churches. As a result, those that are compelled to wait are doing so in vain as our churches continue to dwindle.

Marriage continues to preoccupy the minds of all—rich or poor, young or old. It is this preoccupation that sends people that are not quite ready for marriage to the altar. An institution this universal has surprisingly few prerequisites. It requires more work to do just about anything else, obtain a driver's license, enter into a competitive field of work, buy a home, get a college degree. Marriage, on the other hand, requires only four things: a state ID, $45, 1 or 2 witnesses, and somebody authorized to officiate.

The ease of obtaining a legally sanctioned marriage should be a red flag for those of us in the clergy. We must encourage couples considering marriage to slow down and invest in premarital counseling. If they are willing to spend thousands of dollars and months of preparation and angst agonizing over the minutia of wedding details, why shouldn't they be willing to invest time and energy into ensuring that the event isn't a wasted effort? They should be setting themselves up for success, which is far more important than a beautiful wedding.

The sad reality is that many couples maintain that they just do not have the time, that 1.5 hours a week for 10 weeks is too much of a commitment. Others complain that the cost for counseling doesn't fit into their budget. It is no wonder so many marriages falter.

The flowers, the dress, the cake, the expensive food all will fade from memory. This, of course, is not to deter lovers from making the best of their wedding day. Bring the poetry, the revelry, bring the music and the gourmet food. Bring the beautiful flower arrangements and the exuberant wedding party. Bring the romance. But in all this, in the intimate space of the counseling space, bring your bodies, hearts, minds, and faith to discover skills and tools that you will need for survival after the music stops and the wedding guests have gone home.

Pastors and wedding officiants should set some basic requirements that engaged couples must meet before they will be allowed to marry. Parents who are paying for the wedding should budget not only for the flowers and the food, but also for the counseling sessions. Couples should prioritize their time and ensure that they speak with a competent marriage counselor. If your faith community does not have one available, ask around and find one that will do justice to your future. There are many things that you will play Russian roulette with in your life—your marriage should not be one of them.

Premarital What? The Resistant Partner

So, you have decided to get engaged, and the one carat princess cut diamond you saved months, if not years, for sits proudly on her finger. She looks at it a dozen times a day; it is almost as if she is checking to make sure it is still there. Next comes in the seemingly interminable barrage of questions. What date will you set? How many people will be invited? Vera Wang or couture? Roses or lilies for the centerpieces? How about the bridal party? Destination wedding or honeymoon in Aruba? The answers will barely be out of your mouth before the next obvious line of questioning begins.

When will you get pregnant? How many do you want? Our thinking is very linear when it comes to starting a family. Our views on how life should progress are deeply rooted in our culture and traditions. This movement is usually thus: engagement, wedding, marriage, children, retirement.

Startlingly, and perhaps counterintuitively, there is usually no mention of premarital counseling in this lineup. I have sat with many a hopeful bride or groom who have lamented that their significant other does not see the need for counseling. I have also seen responsible, mature partners insist on receiving premarital counseling. Without being too hard on my brothers, you are more likely to resist counseling than your better halves. It is also true that, after marriage, women often lament that their husbands think that talking with a pastor or counselor will not improve anything. Many men have a deep seated, underlying fear of feelings. Feelings are too feminine, too "soft." Even in full-blown crisis, men generally do not feel that outside intervention is necessary, tending instead to view counseling as a threat. They think that the preacher will be too preachy; s/he will side with their spouse; s/he will try to convert them or make them feel ashamed.

Unfortunately, the clergy continues to perpetuate this dynamic of suspicion and mistrust. There is a desperate need for competent, professional pastoral marriage and family counselors. Effective premarital counseling enables couples to:

- develop realistic expectations of marriage,
- better understand each other,

- resolve lingering conflicts that should not enter the marriage space,
- develop communication and problem-solving skills that can be applied to future conflicts and,
- confront taboo issues such as sex, power, money, in-laws, and politics.

When a partner is unwilling to try counseling, it is important to understand the root of the resistance. If it is based on the idea that the counselor won't be unbiased, reassure him/her that the role of any respectable counselor is to be neutral. If the counselor is closer to one of the partners, s/he should acknowledge that in the first session. Further, if impartiality is impossible, the counselor should step aside and recommend another. If your partner is afraid that private matters will surface, the counselor should reassure the couple by reminding them of the confidentiality rule.

Mentoring Couples: A Dying Resource

Sometime ago, my wife and I joined a Facebook group for married couples where people engage in conversation, raise questions, and post inspirational quotes about marriage. Often, serious issues arise—sick children, aging parents, and conflict management to name a few. This online community is one way that couples connect with other couples to find support in building and sustaining their marriages. The internet enables couples to broaden their scope of connection, becoming part of a larger community of people with similar concerns.

In chapter one, we learned that the nuclear family cannot be entirely self-sufficient. It needs the support of the extended family, friends, and the community. The same thing goes for married couples. Complete autonomy isn't possible in a healthy marriage. Couples need to link with other couples for mentoring, support, and accountability. The age of privacy has caused a ripple effect of isolation that is predominant today. Individuals are isolated from their families, families are isolated from their communities, communities are isolated from each other. This isolation has left husbands and wives feeling lonely and unsupported, especially when those marriages are not stable. The two extremes of such isolation are Us vs. Them and Me vs. You.

- *Us vs. Them* — Couples, especially young couples, often see themselves as partners against the world. This is a romantic notion, and an entirely naive and unrealistic one. It's also not what God intended. How do I know this? Well, because of Ruth and Boaz, Abraham and Sarah, David and Abigail. Extended families are still essential, friendships still matter, your community is still important. While marriage may redefine other relationships, it should never restrict or damage them. Most especially, it should not eliminate them.

- *Me vs. You* — In this instance, spouses are at odds with each other. They don't feel they can turn to others for support because they believe marriage means that other close relationships are dissolved or minimized once they're married. Hence, couples don't turn to family, friends, or counselors in times of crisis. They are distrustful of counseling and seldom turn to extended family members, viewing them as incidental, existing only in their periphery. With all these neglected resources, couples are bound to find themselves in trouble with no way out.

Mike and Harriet McManus are Christians who have developed a successful program called Marriage Savers designed to prepare people for marriage, strengthen marriages that are already functional, and restore marriages that are on the verge of collapsing. Mature, established couples within faith communities mentor and support couples in distress, newlyweds, and young couples among others. The program provides human capital, educational, and therapeutic support for couples. It invites us to reimagine what support looks like. Marriage counseling can be overrated, and, yes, I speak as a marriage counselor. In fact, I would argue that many of the struggles that we face can be remediated within a community setting. I do not mean to imply that there is no place for more formal counseling in a structured setting. Counselors provide an invaluable service to those seeking emotional assistance. Yet, familial relationships can often help mediate a crisis in a quicker and more organic way.

Often, my wife and I are invited to a couple's home for dinner. We sit close to each other, eat, drink, laugh, and even have some serious conversations. We are committed to our friends, and they are committed to us. If one of those relationships hit hard times, there is a good chance that my wife will get a call to say, "Hey, can we talk a bit?" We husbands can expect that one of us will reach out to say, "What's going on, my brother?" We know that the support is there without ever even asking. It is this kind of mentoring relationship that I am advancing here. Embedded within it is a connection that is beyond the dyad, one that offers support during hard times and is accountable to the larger community.

Many become nervous when they hear the term "accountability." It is a word that evokes feelings of guilt, blame, and even hostility. But, in the case of mentoring marriages, accountability is not about finger-pointing or judgment. Rather, it is about husbands and wives checking in with one another, offering support and encouragement to work out differences in ways that strengthen their marriage. I know that this kind of nonthreatening accountability works because I have seen what happens to marriages when such support is peeled away. I have also seen how marriages thrive when this level of support is fully intact.

Community of Couples: A New Way of Understanding Support Groups

The age of individualism has separated person from family, family from community, the community from the global, and humanity from the

Divine. In Community: The Structure of Belonging, Peter Block argues, "The social fabric of community is formed from an expanding shared sense of belonging. It is shaped by the idea that only when we are connected and care for the well-being of the whole that a civil and democratic society is created."[11] Partners can strengthen their marriage by connecting with other couples—both in and out of their faith communities—who share similar values and beliefs. I'm convinced that when couples are estranged from the community as well as from other couples, their marriages are more susceptible to breakdown. Those who belong to a community of other couples can rely on that social network for support during difficult times. They can also learn from the wisdom and experiences of others who've been through similar situations. I have noted elsewhere in this book that therapeutic relationships are all around us. Professional therapists do not have the market cornered on what it means to offer social and emotional support.

When couples are isolated from the community, daily challenges escalate into more serious issues that can threaten the very health and wellbeing of couples. Belonging to a community of couples means that support is always there. Other couples can answer questions, give counsel, encourage, and even just be there to listen. I have seen too many times

---

[11] Peter Block, *Community: The Structure of Belonging*, Oakland: Berrett-Koehler Publishers, 2008.

that when couples are isolated, they become victims of their own circumstances. Here are some ways that couples can form social networks to strengthen their marriages:

1. Game nights with other couples deepen trusting relationships. They can be used as tools to access taboo areas and surface issues such as communication, conflict resolution, etc.

2. Group date nights such as going to dinner and a movie can help to build community.

3. Well planned retreats can also help couples bond with each other.

4. Other couples can serve as mediators during times of conflict.

Most of us interact with other couples on some level. Sometimes, with a little tweaking, we can harness resources from our social network to build and sustain healthy marriages. When healthy and intentional, these networks not only serve to strengthen our marriages, they can become the ties that bind. I invite you to do a rapid social network inventory to find married couples that you interact with relatively frequently. Make connections with couples that you know and trust, ones you can turn to for specific support. For example, which couple would you be able to turn to if you are dealing with infertility? Or, which couple might you look to for support in dealing with a difficult teenager? If you are dealing with infidelity, is there a couple who might be able to offer advice? What about financial disagreements?

In short, it's not just having access to other trusted couples during difficult times. Some of those couples may have knowledge and resources that can support us. Together, we can give each other the tools and human capital necessary to access such resources.

Reflection: Your Social Network

1. Consider 3-5 couples in your circle of friends and family that you and your significant other can reach out to for support during relational conflict.

2. What are some qualities you see in those couples that you think might strengthen your own marriage and vice versa?

3. What are their jobs? How can their expertise support you and your family?

4. What might prevent you from seeking the support of other couples?

5. Can you think of other sources that you can tap into for wise and life-giving advice about working on overcoming differences in your marriage or relationship?

Question 3 can serve an important role in bringing value to your life. For example, if your child is struggling in school and one of those individuals is a principal, s/he can possibly negotiate services for your child. Someone who has overcome infidelity can bring hope to your marriage during a tumultuous and uncertain time. None of us should live outside of community. Many churches and social networks do great work in creating circles of support for each other even in informal spaces such as couples' get togethers, anniversaries, and birthday celebrations.

Finding Your Story in Scripture — Jacob and Rachel (Gen 29)

Talk about long courtships! Jacob loved Rachel so much, he worked for seven years to prove it. As you read their story, consider the depth of Jacob's love. If you aren't half as committed as he was, if you wouldn't sacrifice even a quarter of the time he did to earn his bride, you may want to reevaluate your reasons for wanting to get married. Consider premarital counseling—please. Marriage is forever. Is your commitment?

Strengthening the Ties that Bind	Helpful Resources
"Pastors and wedding officiants should set some basic requirements that engaged couples must meet before they will be allowed to marry. Parents who are paying for the wedding should budget not only for the flowers and the food, but also for the counseling sessions. Couples should prioritize their time and ensure that they speak with a competent marriage counselor."	Marriage Mentoring Curriculum Marriagementoring.com

Northeast Region Marriage and Family Retreats http://www.cogopner.org/married-couples.html

Montefiore Healthy Relationships Program https://www.montefiore.org/supporting-healthy-relationships

Relationship and Marriage Education Network fcs.uga.edu/nermen

Marriage Savers: http://www.marriagesavers.org/ Contact Marriage Savers at 301-978-7108 or Mike@marriagesavers.org for information about training.

Marriage Mentoring: 12 Conversations http://www.12conversations.com/

PREPARE https://www.prepare-enrich.com

American Addiction Centers: https://americanaddictioncenters.org/rehab-guide/christian |

IV

DIVORCE AND BREAK-UPS: A FACT OF LIFE

Never allow someone to be your priority while allowing yourself to be their option."
— Mark Twain

The Case of Andy and Jade

Andy and Jade were high school sweethearts. After high school, they both enrolled in a local public college. Andy majored in Economics; Jade in Education. They went on to pursue graduate degrees from separate online programs. Throughout their secondary and post-secondary education, they dated exclusively. Ultimately, both obtained full-time work in their respective fields. They were ready to take their relationship to the next level—marriage. Deciding to skip a long engagement, they had a simple wedding in Jade's parents' backyard with about 30 close friends and family. Andy's grandfather, a non-denominational pastor, officiated.

When asked about premarital counseling, Jade said it wasn't necessary since they had been together for their entire adolescent and adult lives and knew each other inside and out. They also felt that, while they did have some communication issues, they were mature enough to handle them without third party intervention.

Their relationship began to show signs of trouble just two years into the marriage. Jade worked for an inner city charter school that demanded 10-hour work days. Because she often brought work home with her, ten hours would turn into twelve or more as she became preoccupied with email, grading papers, lesson planning, and other administrative responsibilities. Although stressed and overworked, she never complained and remained dedicated to her students and her responsibilities.

Andy had a time consuming job as well. His position at a demanding company required that he be in the office for 8-10 hours a day and on the road several days a week. He pushed himself to work even longer hours in order to save for early retirement. He was ultimately offered a VP position. While this came with a significant salary increase, it unfortunately also meant that he would be home even less. Although Jade was happy for him, she was concerned that they were drifting apart and that this promotion would only alienate them further. Though they agreed to make an effort to spend time together, their focus remained on their careers.

After six months in his new position, Andy asked if Jade would consider quitting her job since he was making more than enough money. Jade was shocked and hurt that he would ask her to leave a job she was clearly passionate about. When probed, Andy said, "Well, we don't need the money and I am concerned about how stressed out you have been lately. You seem listless and unhappy with your job. They seem to demand more and give less." Jade reluctantly agreed that she was nearing burn-out and needed to consider some changes, yet balked at the idea of staying home indefinitely. Her alternative suggestion was to use the summer to try to get into the local public school, which had union protection, tenure opportunity, and shorter hours. Not convinced, Andy insisted that she give some more thought to his proposal.

Jade decided to broach the subject of children—or, rather, their lack of—a decision largely made by Andy. She would consider staying home if he was also willing to revisit the idea of having a baby. She was only 20 when they decided against having kids, she reminded him. At 29, she was beginning to feel differently. Unmoved, Andy replied, "Well, I feel the same way today as I did a decade ago." His refusal to consider her needs left Jade feeling hurt and resentful. She realized that premarital counseling would have allowed her to voice her feelings about any ambivalence she may have had about not having children.

A year passed. Jade gave up her job and stayed home. She enjoyed having financial security and volunteered two days a week at a local high school doing SAT prep. However, this was not enough to keep the anxiety over her struggling marriage at bay. After having several panic attacks, she decided to seek counseling. In her therapy sessions, she opened up about her dissatisfaction with her marriage and discovered that her desire for *children was nonnegotiable. She also realized how angry and resentful she was at being coerced into giving up her career.*

Meanwhile, Andy's dissatisfaction with his marriage coupled with long hours at the office led to an intense sex affair with his assistant, Kate. She soon discovered that she was pregnant. Distraught, Andy begged her to terminate the pregnancy, but she refused. She told him that at 39 she may not get another chance to have a child. She assured him that as long as he handled his financial responsibilities, she would not involve him in the child's life.

Guilt and worry plagued Andy. He began to lose sleep and became distracted and unfocused. Noticing his restlessness and lack of appetite, Jade told herself that her husband was just reacting to their recent fights. When his distress brought him to the hospital with chest pain, she suspected that there was more going on. She finally confronted him and he tearfully admitted to the affair and pregnancy, begging for her forgiveness. Jade was devastated. Numb to his repeated apologies, she immediately left and drove four hours to her parents' house where she could be alone with her grief. After three days, she asked her father to secure a lawyer for her and on the fourth day she filed for divorce.

When we fall in love and/or get married, we generally don't plan on the relationship failing. Most people cling to the hope that true love exists, that this relationship will last, that they have finally found "the one." In our quest for a soulmate, however, we tend to overlook the fact that our relationships will fail if we don't nurture them.

I do not believe in soulmates, though my conservative contemporaries will rebuke me for this. Nevertheless, I take a more progressive stance on the issue of finding a mate. I counsel people to date both within and outside of their ethnicity and within and outside of their religious denomination. Said another way, remain open to what God might have in store for you. By restricting yourself to one ethnic group or one denomination you significantly limit your options. In most faith communities, men are outnumbered by women by a significant margin. There simply aren't enough Mr. Rights to go around. Seeking a mate beyond church borders becomes unavoidable. The notion that there is only one person for you also subliminally tells people that they don't need to work on their relationships. But, marriage is like anything else in this world. If you neglect it, you will pay a steep price. But if you nurture it, then it will bear untold fruits. Jade and Andy had a number of challenges that they did not attend to. Their story is, unfortunately, a sad reality for many couples. What can we learn by examining their story?

The Warning Signs Were There

I have a thing about driving my car when the gas is almost on empty. As soon as the yellow light comes on, I break into a cold sweat as I am plagued with visions of trudging down a deserted highway with only the tumbleweeds and thoughts of murderous outlaws to keep me company. My wife thinks I am a being paranoid. Go figure. But, here's why that mocking yellow light is such a problem for me: I have no way of knowing just how much gas is left in the tank. Add to this the fact that New York City traffic is capricious at best and you have a recipe for disaster. I get anxious just thinking about it. To keep my stress level down, I don't let the gauge fall below a half tank. Neuroses aside, there is a lesson here. The truth is that warning signs that our relationship is in trouble are usually right in front of us, but we tend to tune them out or dismiss them as mere annoyances.

I cannot emphasize strongly enough how important it is to pay attention to the warning signs that your marriage is at risk. Andy and Jade started out strong. They supported each other's dreams and worked in tandem building what, by all accounts, would have been a bright future. However, Jade's confidence in herself and her marriage was eroded by an imbalance of power and general lack of communication. More, they devoted the bulk of their time to their careers leaving precious little for enriching their bond as a married couple.

Research shows that people who live together before marriage report a different sense of self after the wedding day. While Andy drowned himself in his work, he left his marriage neglected and starved. What's more, his overbearing and controlling tendencies didn't allow his wife to express her feelings on critical matters such as the decision to have children. This served to widen an already growing chasm between them. Controlling individuals are often unable to see the impact of their behaviors on others. Because of this, they don't understand why their spouse has become bitter and resentful. Andy simply does not see that the distance separating him and his wife largely stems from her growing frustration over her powerlessness.

Marriage Should Be an Equal Partnership

Because of Andy's domineering and narcissistic personality, he thought it was perfectly acceptable to ask Jade to give up her job even though it was her passion. While she did feel stressed about work, giving up her career was not the answer. What she needed from her husband was support and encouragement, not "solutions" that invalidated her need for fulfillment outside of their marriage. What Andy failed to appreciate was that as a new teacher, Jade was still learning how to pace herself. Most teachers find their stride within the first five years of their careers. Andy did not give Jade that chance. He simply did not feel her career was important enough to warrant any sacrifices or compromises on his part, no matter how temporary.

Andy's needs again eclipsed Jade's when he shut down the conversation about becoming parents. For many women, motherhood is a basic component to their identity and feelings of self-worth. By taking the possibility of children off the table, Andy was effectively letting Jade know that her need for fulfillment in this fundamental area was irrelevant.

A marriage is a contract between two equal parties. Jade's needs were just as valid as Andy's. Yet, he silenced her voice when he refused to give her needs any consideration. It is no surprise that she began to doubt her value and pull away from her husband. Andy's overbearing nature and unreasonable demands created a rift in their marriage they would have been unable to mend without third party mediation.

The dysfunction would eventually take a toll on both of them. Jade's mental health took a beating as her anxiety level rose, while Andy sought comfort in the arms of another. Ironically, the very thing he wanted to prevent happened anyway—fatherhood.

The stark and unyielding language of Eph 5:23—"For the husband is the head of the wife, even as Christ is the head of the church: and he is the savior of the body"—has engendered the unfortunate misinterpretation that women are somehow inferior and men must employ a dictatorial mien in his household. In order to arrive at a fairer and, dare I say, more accurate interpretation of this verse, we must be able to define its language. Precisely, what does it mean to "be the head"? To find our answer, we must examine the following:

- What does headship look like in terms of behavior? Is it life giving?
- How does headship promote an egalitarian marriage?
- Who is in possession of the power in headship?
- If symbolically the man is the head, then symbolically what is the woman?

Whether or not Jade and Andy loved each other is not in dispute. They absolutely did. But, love alone wasn't enough to sustain their marriage. A strong marriage is one of partnership. It is intimate, trusting, and attentive. An imbalanced relationship will almost always encounter setbacks and difficulties. The subordinate party faces low self-esteem and feelings of resentment.

Right now, I am writing this from a spacious suite in a posh hotel in Sydney, Australia on the invitation of my wife. As I write, I think back to one summer several years ago, when our family returned home from a camp up in Maine. As my wife played the answering machine, one particular message got our attention. "Hello Senikha, I am calling from TIAA-CREF regarding your recent application. Give me a call at your convenience to set up an interview...." I encouraged her to call back immediately. Ten years later she has done exceptionally well in the company. I have been her biggest cheerleader. When her job required that she travel across the country, I told her to go for it. When they asked her to travel to Canada, I helped her pack. When they asked her to travel to London, I said, "Take me with you!"

Now, here we are in Australia. My wife's success made this possible. Had ours not been a marriage between equals it is unlikely we'd be here. The saying, "behind every great man is a great woman" doesn't ring true in my estimation. I want my wife beside me, not behind me. In your own marriage, I encourage you to embrace a headship that is encouraging rather than restrictive. A strong marriage has as its foundation the principles of partnership and equality.

I was a student for most of our marriage. My wife stuck by me when I was an undergrad, grad student, and doctoral candidate even though it meant that between school and my full-time job, she would have to take up the slack in parenting and domestic duties. She watched with pride as I received my high school diploma, bachelor's degree, two master's degrees, and my Ph.D. I am now working on my third master's and she is still pushing me along. From working with me on this project, co-facilitating workshops, traveling with me at home and abroad, she has been more than a partner, she is my biggest champion.

Our lives have been intertwined for so long, it's hard to imagine where I'd be without her love and support. I consult her on everyday decisions as much as I use her as a sounding board for gut wrenching ones. The times when I don't feel her support are rare; on those days, I tend to lose sleep. Those are also the days that I am likely to do some deep soul searching. I accept her objections and concerns because there is no part of me that questions her intentions as coming from any place other than genuine love for me and our family. In those instances, I am quick to examine myself, not her motives.

Sensitivity to the Needs of the Other

While Jade and Andy both felt alone in their marriage, they responded to this feeling differently. Jade became increasingly distressed emotionally and sought help through therapy. There, she was able to find validation of her feelings. Andy took comfort in the arms of another woman. Neither was sensitive to the needs of their partner. Their lives became the proverbial two ships passing in the night. They became so steeped in their own suffering, they failed to see that the other was in pain, too.

I once read a quote that said you could be in a library by yourself and never feel alone. You can also be in a crowded room and feel utterly alone and worse, lonely. Marriage was always meant to remove both loneliness and aloneness. To be with another person and feel alone in some ways can feel worse than not having anyone. In Genesis, God said, "it is not good for a man to be alone" and so woman was created to be his partner. She was equal in substance as demonstrated by Adam's confession, "This is now bone of my bones and flesh of my flesh; she shall be called 'woman,' for she was taken out of man" (Gen 2:23). Adam's words drive home the fact that the woman is made of the same raw materials as man. She is equal in substance to man in the eyes of God. Men should remember Adam's words and choose to view marriage as a covenant between God and two equal partners.

There is a story about a man who spent years in the wilderness. He suffered both brutal heat and frostbite, was bitten by all sorts of creatures, and nearly starved. When asked what was the most difficult part of his ordeal, his response was not having any human contact. I often think about those who live in isolation. What must it be like for them to be deprived of the warmth of basic touch? It's impossible to measure the value of a simple embrace. These days, we are hyper-sensitive about our personal space and are leery about touching others. Another unfortunate marker of the times is a pervasive skepticism that has settled over our society. An untrusting culture, we are more likely to regard each other with suspicion, choosing instead to believe the worst of other people. Ours is an age of rampant litigiousness and opportunism. In the interest of self-preservation, the easiest solution is to avoid physical contact altogether.

Sweeping "It" under the Rug Does Not Make the House Clean

In The Seven Principles for Making Marriage (2015), John Gottman argues that he can predict which marriages will fail and which will succeed based on the ratio of positive to negative interactions between partners. He notes that for there to be any hope for couples, every negative interaction must have at least five positive ones. For this next activity, think about a random day in your marriage. Consider the number of negative vs. positive interactions.

Activity: Tabulating Negative vs. Positive Interactions

- How did you both start out your day? Was it with "good morning" or with some form of negative encounter?
- What kindness(es) did you extend to each other?
- Did you carry over a fight from the day before?
- What unsettled conflict continues to preoccupy your thinking and your interactions with each other?

Next, consider which of those interactions could have been avoided and how quickly you were able to resolve and move past them. How might you have handled those differently?

Think about 5-8 times during that day when you might have missed an opportunity to engage in a positive interaction such as paying a compliment, saying thank you etc. Gottman is right, it's not in the explosive moments or in the knock-down, drag-out fights that marriage is destroyed— all couples have huge blow-ups and then return to loving and lovemaking. Rather, marriages are irreparably fractured in the subtle yet systematic injuries of disrespect, emotional isolation, and tuning each other out. Conversely, marriage is sustained and strengthened by making each decision, resolving each conflict, and overcoming each obstacle together and with careful deliberation. Each successful resolution builds resilience in the marriage.

Some time ago, I had a lingering flu that just wouldn't go away. Every time I thought I was over it, I would wake up feeling as though someone had run me over the night before. I rested as best as I could, took flu medicine and drank lots of tea; still, the symptoms persisted. I finally dragged myself to the doctor who told me that my immune system just needed a little push in the right direction and gave me a five-day course of antibiotics. He explained that the medicine would build up in my system and stay there for about 12 days. In many ways, positive interactions are like antibiotics. The effects of its kind last long after the acts themselves. The effects of hostility and conflict, on the other hand, are cumulative. In the movie The Hobbit, Lady Galtria asks Gandolf why he chose Bilbo Baggins to be the champion against evil. His reply is as meaningful as it is timeless: "Saroman believes that it is only great powers that can hold evil in check, but ... I have found that it's the small things, everyday deeds of ordinary folk that keeps the darkness at bay. Simple acts of kindness and love..."

I have often said that if men and women exercise goodness, many tragedies could be avoided. The same is true in relationships. If we expend more energy being kind to each other, more marriages would thrive and the divorce rate would decrease. An irreconcilable difference is another word for obstinacy or, better yet, an unwavering unwillingness to compromise or forgive. Families ought to exercise kindness towards each other in their everyday interactions. Here are some simple things we can say to each other to build sustainable family relationships:

- Thank you.
- I am sorry.
- I promise to do better.
- It was not your fault.
- I should have chosen my words more wisely.
- That didn't come out right, what I really meant to say was...
- Tell me how you would prefer to be addressed.
- I know that you are upset, but I am not sure why. Can you please share your heart with me so that I know what you are feeling?
- That food was amazing! Thanks for cooking my favorite.

- I know you didn't have to put in the extra time at work. I know you did it because we are pressed for money. I really appreciate your effort.
- Why don't we order out tonight rather than cooking?

Marriage works not because people are "meant to be," and families thrive not because our relationships are perfect. They thrive because in our ordinary exchanges, we choose to be kind and compassionate towards each other. We thrive when we are willing to cede our own needs for the needs of the whole. Indeed we thrive when we put Christ at the center of our longing and belonging. If it is "the small foxes that spoil the vines" then it is the small moments that build the whole.

Reflection

1. Adam spoke to his wife about the fact that they were made from the same substance by God to live, work, and procreate in the same house (garden). How can we return to this concept of being made by God for each other to strengthen our relationships?

2. The case study presents a young married couple who has drifted apart. Who do you relate to the most, and why?

3. What might be one question you would ask them? One area of celebration? One piece of advice for this couple?

4. Pain is personal and experienced through one's own senses. Can you think of a time when your own pain prevented you from empathizing with someone else? How did you cross over to bear witness or move past your own pain to help someone else?

Finding Your Story in Scripture — Divorce in the Old and New Testament

Many people wonder why the God of the Old Testament would allow divorce (Deut 24:1-4) but Jesus disdains it (Mark 10:11-12). Well, if you look carefully at Jesus' words in Matthew 19:8, you'll notice that he says that Moses allowed divorce because of the "hardness of your hearts." When we were little kids, our parents gave us rules even though they weren't ultimately the rules that we were going to live by as adults—limiting internet and tv access, only allowing two cookies after dinner, setting curfews, etc. Why? Because children don't have great impulse control or self-discipline, and they are still developing their morality.

When Moses gave the Law, the Israelites were still kids. They were still learning how to be God's chosen. Remember, Moses gave that law to a people who had been slaves in a foreign, pagan country for 400 years. That's plenty of time to develop some pretty bad ethics. Allowing divorce may very well have been a concession to prevent something worse from happening, like a husband deciding to off his wife just to be rid of the burden.

In the New Testament, the training wheels are off. Jesus is calling us to be better, to circumcise our hearts (Rom 2:28-29), and live as God meant before it got all messed up in the Garden of Eden one fateful day. As Christians of the New Covenant, we must rise above the old law and embrace the new. I'm not going to lie, it's definitely harder. But, the reward is so much greater. Isn't it time to grow up?

Strengthening the Ties that Bind	Helpful Resources
"We cannot control the family we are born into. The children of Prince William did not ask to be born into Britain's royal family. Neither did the child born to the teenage mother and father in Harlem or the child of the young mother living in a hut in the slums of Johannesburg ask for their lot in life."	Divorcecare.org "DivorceCare is a friendly, caring group of people who will walk alongside you through one of life's most difficult experiences. Don't go through separation or divorce alone." Divorce Care For Kids: https://www.dc4k.org/

V

SEX RECLAIMED AS LIFE GIVING

I am a man, I consider nothing that is human alien to me.
—Terence

We are sexual beings; God made us that way. Sexual activity strengthens the bonds of marriage by deepening intimacy. It makes us vulnerable to our spouse while inspiring trust and exclusivity. Although it can be a bit uncomfortable and, at times, volatile, the topic of sex and sexuality must be addressed transparently if faith communities are to effectively combat a number of issues—women with children from multiple partners, men who are not willing to commit to one partner or care for the children they produce, an increased divorce rate, the dissolution of relationships between cohabiting couples, and teenage pregnancy to name a few.

Our perceptions of sex and sexuality are complex and multi-layered, ranging from the utilitarian to the epicurean, the sacred to the depraved. William F. May[12] discusses four prevailing views of sex:

1. Sex as divine
2. Sex as a casual encounter
3. Sex as a chore
4. Sex as dirty and devilish

---

[12] William F. May, "Four Mischievous Theories of Sex: Demonic, Divine, Casual, and Nuisance," *Perspectives on Marriage: A Reader* 3 (2007): 186-95.

I would add a fifth and sixth view—sex as a commodity and sex as a means of power and control.

Sex as Divine

Some of my theologian friends are quick to elevate sex between a husband and wife into the heavenlies. They claim that sex is a gift from God (which I agree with) and that having sex with your spouse is ministry. For them, sex is a spiritual experience, a duty, a call into ministry with our spouses. While I am fascinated by this theology, I can't say that I am completely sold on it, nor am I interested in dismissing it altogether. Of all the views presented in this chapter, it is the only one that isn't "bruising," or non-life giving. Sex as divine invites us to live our sexual lives with integrity, honor, self-control, and within the covenantal space of holy matrimony. Additionally, sex is best understood as a gift from God that is intricately and inseparably linked to:

- The deepest way of understanding what it means to be one flesh
- An expression of vulnerability, unity, and a shared commitment to pursuing happiness and pleasure
- Strengthening the relationship through intimacy
- Have basic human needs met within the covenantal space

In a world where sex is bought, sold, used as leverage, and used as a means of power and control, we would do well to embrace this view of sex as divine, however lofty it might be. While there is plenty of room to debate the pitfalls of elevating sex to such a glorified level, we would do well to view sex through a more Godly lens. When we embrace the idea that sex is a gift from God, we can situate our conversations and values regarding children that are conceived through planned and unplanned pregnancies and their right to life. Sex as a divine gift explains why the act requires synergy between body, mind, and emotion and can serve as a glue that helps to hold our unions together. Finally, it legitimizes the need to speak candidly about the importance of not allowing the stresses and distractions of the world to interfere with healthy sexual activity between spouses.

Sex as a Casual Encounter

Many people have sex without a commitment beyond the act itself. Casual sex is so commonplace, in fact, that we have a plethora of idioms to describe it: 'friends with benefits,' 'hooking up,' and 'no strings attached,' are just a few.

All sorts of reasons exist as to why casual sex is dangerous for both the heart and the body. Therapists tell us that many people engage in casual sex because of a disordered notion of love and affection that is the result of learned behaviors in childhood which send us seeking pleasure without commitment. Theologians tell us that it's our Adamic nature magnified. Even the most righteous of us is not immune to temptation. 2 Samuel 2 tells how when King David saw a beautiful woman taking a bath, he was so captivated by her that he went to her immediately and had sex with her (likely giving her little choice). When she wound up pregnant, David murdered her husband in order to have her for himself.

Sociologists tell us that when social expectations and boundaries erode, there's a proliferation of people engaging in sexual activity without any concern about future commitment. They tell us this is also in part because of the weakening influence of religious institutions, laws, and social norms on the family system. Religious leaders and clergy members tell us that every time you have sex with a person you take on their spirit, you bind yourself to them. Thus, each sexual encounter opens you up to spiritual attack.[13]

The problem with casual sex is that it opens the door for consequences that both parties might not be prepared to deal with. Take, for example, a casual, commitment-free encounter that results in a child. The babe is unwanted, was not produced in love, and has parents that are unaccountable to each other. That poor child's future is bleak. Or, consider a casual tryst that results in one partner infecting the other with a disease. Casual encounters cheapen the meaning of sex and reduce the human body to merely a means to an end—pleasure.

---

[13] Though I am wary of this type of thinking as it can lead to fanaticism, it is still worth noting.

Sex as a Chore

Most of us don't like chores. They are time consuming, repetitive, and tiring—necessary evils, if you will. Believe it or not, some feel this way about sex; they get it done, roll over and go to sleep. For them, technique, mood, and ambiance are irrelevant. Foreplay is unnecessary. There is no finesse, no intimate conversation, and no deeper meaning to lovemaking. For a spouse with a high sex drive this is the ultimate frustration, not just because the bedroom is often cold and boring, but because sex becomes a one-way encounter. The excited and energized spouse after a while begins to feel that the act is exclusively for him/herself. His/her partner puts in minimum effort, does not appear to be enjoying it, and has little or nothing to say before, during, or after sex.

It's not fair, however, to lay the blame solely at the feet of the reticent partner. People need to feel appreciated, wanted, sexy, desirable. They don't want to feel like a piece of meat. The eager partner should take pains to ensure s/he is doing everything possible to make the experience good for both parties. It might be that the reluctant spouse is responding to the rushed partner who enjoys the act itself but not the preamble. The over-eager party may need to slow down, take a moment, and respond to the needs of his/her spouse.

A person's libido can be mitigated by many different factors: stress, depression, illness, and fatigue all impact our sexual desire. This is why it's critical that we have open dialogue about our sex life. In counseling, I often have couples grade their level of satisfaction in the bedroom (without showing their answer to their partner). This activity, while it can produce some anxiety, fosters open dialogue about something that couples tend to avoid discussing. I ask them: *On a scale of 1-10, how would you rate your satisfaction in the bedroom? Ideally how many times a week would you want to have sex?*

I then ask them to consider their partner's wants and needs. This can be a bit daunting. No one wants to think that their partner is unsatisfied sexually. Nevertheless, in a healthy marriage, both spouses must feel sexually fulfilled. That's why the next two questions in this activity are crucial. *On a scale of 1-10, how would your spouse rate his/her satisfaction in the bedroom? Ideally, how many times a week would you say your spouse wants to make love?*

When the answers to these questions elicit surprise, chagrin, or disagreement, I encourage couples to explore the reasons for this and imagine solutions. Why do you think your answers might be similar or different from your spouse? *What are some reasons why your ideal frequency of weekly sexual activities might be different from your spouse? What might you both do to address these differences?*

If this activity is approached with openness, honesty, and trust it can be very revelatory. Couples are often shocked to discover how far apart they are with their answers. When sex becomes merely an obligation, it, like so many obligations, becomes a source of resentment which will widen the distance separating the couple.

Keeping the Fire Alive

Successful marriages require time and effort, including frequent intimate encounters with your spouse. Don't be afraid to mix it up. Long, slow nights of passion are indisputably incredible, but don't write off the "quickie" before work in the morning. Those can be just as much fun. Sex is work, but it's good work. We need not discuss all the physical, emotional, and spiritual benefits of a healthy sex life. Suffice it to say, without consistent affection, couples tend to have more frequent fights, be out of sync with each other, and generally behave less kindly towards one another. The healthier our sex lives, the more we think about—and think fondly of—each other, and the more giving we become. Here are 9 tips for keeping the fire alive:

1. Talk to each other about how you are doing in the bedroom. Make sure you are on the same page, using non-judgmental language.

2. Keep an open mind to hearing dissatisfaction. It's not an indictment against you; your partner has the right and the responsibility to ask for more and so do you – within safe and comfortable parameters.

3. Schedule time to make love. Spontaneity is great except that you don't know when or IF its going to happen. Do short getaways, date nights, and staycations.

4. Touch each other often even if it doesn't lead to sex. An affirming touch is a positive encounter.

5. Mix it up. Have long romantic foreplays, intense, and protracted sex, but also have quickies that get the job done for the both of you. The bed is undefiled.

6. Be creative. Try new positions in new places with new tools. Don't be afraid to be adventurous. Again, the bed is undefiled. Just make sure you are both comfortable. Consider having a safe word.

7. Compliment each other. Praise your spouse before, during, and after sex and you will be surprised how far it will get the both of you. Speaking negatively about body size, performance, etc. will definitely kill the mood.

8. Exercise patience. Men and women are not always on the same wavelength in the bedroom. Be gentle and supportive with each other during dry spells.

9. Consult your doctor—help is out there.

Sex as Dirty and Devilish

Even today, there are many people who view sex as necessary but intrinsically evil. It is not hard to figure out why. We are inundated on a daily basis with stories of infidelity, promiscuity, sexual deviance, and sex crimes. We are beset by lewd, salacious advertising and an amoral and licentious entertainment industry. Sexual predators are everywhere—in our schools, on the streets, even in our churches. They come into our homes through the internet. They wear the mask of friend, teacher, and relative. Sex is a business; sex is a weapon; sex is an inevitability. The western world is mired in a sexual gluttony so pervasive and insidious it isn't even aware of how deeply its cravings run. It is really no wonder why those seeking a purer ethos, a higher morality, make the improperly ordered judgment that all sex acts are intrinsically evil.

In this age of moral ambivalence, it's important to realize that in and of itself, sex is not dirty or evil. Like anything else, it can be polluted and debased for selfish consumption. While churches have historically been good at framing an anti-sex message, they haven't been as successful at dissuading folks from engaging in sex out of wedlock. Still, we must continue to teach people to live morally while acknowledging that we are sexual beings as much as we are social beings in need of community. When sex is seen as inherently sinful, it impacts and impedes bedroom behaviors. As a pastoral counselor, I frequently have to disabuse married couples of the belief that sexual intimacy is shameful and that engaging in acts of lovemaking is somehow sinful. Many Christians are afraid to explore the depth of their sexuality believing that sex is solely for the purpose of procreation and never for pleasure. This misguided way of thinking is harmful and certainly not what God intended. We need to abandon this puritanical mindset and live authentically, accepting that, as human beings, we have sexual needs.

Sex as a Commodity

When reduced to a commodity, sex is used as a means to exploit the innocent and powerless for financial gain. As long as sex sells, issues such as sex in advertising, prostitution, and human trafficking will continue to be a blight on the human condition.

Sex in Advertising

The advertising industry has been using sex as a marketing tool for nearly a century, if not longer. From subliminal product design and marketing gimmicks to in-your-face television commercials, sex has become the ubiquitous constant that is used to sell nearly everything. Would it surprise you to learn that the iconic Coca-Cola bottle looks the way it does because it mimics a woman's curves? How many of you have found the profile of the naked, aroused man on a box of Camel cigarettes? Numerous cosmetics and personal care items—lipsticks, hair styling products, bath and shower products—come in packaging that ranges from the flirty to the down-right suggestive. Need I remind you of the eyebrow raising Herbal Essence shampoo ads? The clothing industry is unapologetically blatant about using sex in advertising campaigns. If you are over 40, you are undoubtedly familiar with the infamous Calvin Klein campaign in the early '80s that had a semi-nude, very young Brooke Shields claiming, "No one comes between me and my Calvins." Look at many of the magazine and window ads for Abercrombie and Fitch—a popular young adult clothier—and you won't find a stitch of clothing on the models—the extremely well built, visually appealing models. I could easily name a dozen beer and liquor ads that showcase all manner of bikini wearing women in suggestive poses. This is somewhat understandable considering casual sex and alcohol are common bedfellows. But, what are we to make of the more recent trend in advertising that incorporates a sexual message into ads for decidedly unsexy products? A 2013 television commercial for Liquid Plumr shows a housewife answering her front door to two buff plumbers announcing they've arrived to "snake her pipes" and "flush her drain" as she stands there visibly aroused. Sheba cat food marketers came up with the strange idea to use a scantily clad Eva Longoria to convince potential consumers that, what? Buying Sheba for their cats will make cat owners more sexually desirable? And I won't offend anyone's sensibilities by detailing the Poise feminine incontinence ad that uses innuendo and purposely misleading dialogue to link bladder leakage protection with intercourse and ... other things.

As this topic could easily spiral down a rabbit hole, I will briefly conclude by stating what I now hope has become obvious. Sex can be used to sell just about anything. Why? Because we are a people convinced that we are made free by allowing ourselves to do what feels good, whenever and however it comes. The irony, I hope, is evident. When we are ruled by our sexual appetites, we are hardly liberated. And, those who have caught on to the fact that we've deluded ourselves into thinking that we are will exploit us, milking us for every penny we've got.

Prostitution

It's not called the oldest profession for no reason. Some of our most ancient records speak of women who sell their bodies. The Bible records quite a few tales of prostitutes, some reformed, some not. Jesus is, in fact, a descendant of Rahab, the prostitute who hid Joshua's spies from the Canaanites at Jericho. As civilization has become more advanced, prostitution and the buying and selling of sex, which always existed on the fringes of society, has become even more dangerous and deviant. Men and women who turn to prostitution out of desperation (homelessness, addiction, debt) are easily exploited by pimps and other criminals. Often we hear, "It's her body, she can do what she wants with it." But, is this really what anyone truly wants? To have sex with strangers, never knowing if they are dangerous, violent, or carrying diseases? Does any child dream of being a paid escort when she grows up? Unfortunately, the oldest profession isn't likely to ever go out of style. As long as there is desperation and hopelessness in the world there will be those who see prostitution as their only recourse. And sadly, they will never run out of customers.

Human Trafficking

According to the Department of Homeland Security, Human trafficking is "modern-day slavery and involves the use of force, fraud, or coercion to obtain some type of labor or commercial sex act."[14] It should be impossible for hideous crimes like this to happen today, and yet, tragically and shockingly, they do. Women and children are the most frequent victims of human trafficking. Like every market driven economy, there is always someone plotting to profit at someone else's expense.

Impoverished nations are especially susceptible to human trafficking where the "market" for sex is unregulated. Deviants in Western countries looking to purchase individuals for any number of reasons, from sex to forced labor, book flights to dark corners of the world to violate the rights of, and abuse women and children. They then return to their settled cities and suburban lives. In the end, the human person is reduced to a product to be utilized for gains and then discarded when no longer profitable.

Parents must remain vigilant. Don't be lured into a false sense of security because you live in a "nice neighborhood" and "nothing like that could ever happen here." The human trafficking industry is alive and well in the United States. Even if you think such atrocities are highly unlikely, instill a

---

[14] "What is Human Trafficking?" Homeland Security Website, n.d., https://www.dhs.gov/blue-campaign/what-human-trafficking.

healthy wariness and awareness in your children. Be aware of warning signs and indicators of human trafficking:

- Is the person disconnected from family, friends, community organizations, or houses of worship?
- Has a child stopped attending school?
- Has the person had a sudden or dramatic change in behavior?
- Is the person disoriented or confused, or showing signs of mental or physical abuse?
- Does the person have bruises in various stages of healing?
- Is the person fearful, timid, or submissive?
- Does the person show signs of having been denied food, water, sleep, or medical care?
- Is the person often in the company of someone to whom s/he defers? Or someone who seems to be in control of the situation, e.g., where they go or who they talk to?
- Does the person appear to be coached on what to say?
- Is the person living in unsuitable conditions?
- Does the person lack personal possessions and appear not to have a stable living situation?

- Does the person have freedom of movement? Can the person freely leave where they live? Are there unreasonable security measures?[15]

Sex as a Means of Power and Control

There are a number of reasons people engage in sexual activity. This ranges from the most pure, to the most depraved—love, procreation, a desire for intimacy, pleasure, lust, as a means to an end, greed, and to exercise power and control over another. When sex is used to dominate, when it becomes violent and non-consensual, when it is used to extort and terrorize, it is no longer about desirability or even pleasure. It becomes a weapon, no different than any other tool used to intimidate and subjugate.

Rape and Sexual Abuse

In the past, the word 'rape' automatically conjured images of a violent assault perpetrated by an anonymous assailant. While these types of attacks do happen, today we know that rape can occur in a number of situations by many different types of perpetrators—acquaintance rape, date rape, marital rape, statutory rape. There is only one definitive marker for rape, lack of consent. If there is any question about your partner's willingness, err on the side of caution, exercise self-control, and stop what

---

[15] "Indicators of Human Trafficking," Homeland Security Website, n.d., https://www.dhs.gov/blue-campaign/indicators-human-trafficking#.

you're doing. While 'no means no' in every case, it is not the only marker for consent. Children cannot consent, drunk or unconscious people cannot consent, people under obvious duress do not consent. Yes, you can rape your spouse. Yes, you can rape your boyfriend or girlfriend. YES, a man can be raped; and, yes, even by a woman. This is not the platform for an in-depth exploration of rape, abuse, and consent. If you or someone you know has been victimized (even if you are unsure) there are places you can turn to for help. I have listed several at the end of this chapter.

Abuse in the Clergy

People seek solace in a house of worship for any number of reasons:

- because they have been bruised by families, in the workplace, or by society in general,
- for healing,
- to become a part of a community that espouses positive values.

How we treat each other within communities of faith has a direct impact on how we experience the divine. Over the years, I have had some very interesting questions from young children about faith. One keeps reverberating in my mind, "Are you God?" When I reflected on this child's innocent question, I was struck with the realization that ministers have a tremendous amount of power and influence. It humbles me and strengthens my resolve to exercise that power responsibly. Power of course when used for good as Jesus did can make the world over anew. Richard Gula, speaking about pastoral responsibilities and the dangers of dual relationships with our congregants, notes, "The imbalance of power in the pastoral relationship imposes a twofold obligation on the pastoral minister. One is the negative obligation not to use power over others in any way that causes harm. The other is the positive obligation to empower others to become more in charge of their own lives."[16]

Clergy can abuse their power from the pulpit as well as from behind closed doors. Two distinct populations that fall victim to abuse by ministers and church leaders are vulnerable adults and children.

The Abuse of Vulnerable Adults

There can be no consensual sex between vulnerable persons and those in a position of power. Just as an employer cannot have a consensual sexual relationship with an employee, neither can a pastor have a consensual sexual relationship with a member of the congregation. Leaders must not bring sex into their ministerial spaces. They must practice self-discipline with ruthless intentionality to create boundaries and safeguard the faith community against such ties that bruise. Sexual misconduct in these instances has nothing to do with sex and everything to do with the need to exercise power and control over others. When this happens, souls are

---

[16] Richard M. Gula, *Ethics In Pastoral Ministry*. Paulist Press, 1996, 106.

bruised, congregations suffer, and the name of God is desecrated. Servant Leadership must be at the center of the work that we do. We do well in heeding Peter's warning:

> Feed the flock of God which is among you, taking the oversight thereof, not by constraint, but willingly; not for filthy lucre, but of a ready mind; Neither as being lords over God's heritage, but being examples to the flock. And when the chief Shepherd shall appear, ye shall receive a crown of glory that fadeth not away. (I Pet 5:2-4)

If you have been victimized, help is out there. The conclusion of this chapter provides information about where you can go for help. You are not alone. Don't suffer in silence.

The Abuse of Children

Many churches today struggle with what to do when faced with sexual abuse that has been committed by members of its clergy. While working through the decision-making process can be painful and confusing, it should always be guided by a moral imperative to protect the most vulnerable of all—children—which should lead parents, church leaders, and laity to call 911 when there is a suspicion of sexual abuse against a minor. The exploitation of children is not limited to any one religious group. All institutions, including public schools, after-school programs, sports and recreational sectors and, yes, families can have individuals that abuse children. A renewed effort is needed for all clergy and church workers to:

1. Undergo background checks as a prerequisite to working with children
2. Be trained in recognizing signs and symptoms of sexual abuse in minors
3. Know proper organizational protocol and legal responsibility in reporting suspicion of child abuse (including physical and sexual)

The church was always meant to be a reconstructed entity that was designed by God to operate on Biblical principles. Sadly, this is not always so. It is unspeakably tragic, but far too many children and vulnerable adults have been the victims of clergy and church leaders' abuse.

Sexual Harassment

Sexual advances become harassment when they are unwanted. Sexual harassment is any situation in which an employee is made uncomfortable by sexual innuendo, sexual comments and jokes, sexual proposals, or sexual intimidation. We should be hired, promoted, and fired based on the merits of our work not on our ability to acquiesce to sexual advancements or favors in the workplace. We often spend more time with colleagues than we do with our own families. As such, the workplace should be about the work that people are paid to do, not to have to contend with hearing inappropriate innuendoes, remarks, or other physical or emotional violations. Employers should also make it clear to staff and those in leadership roles that sexual or any kind of harassment is strictly prohibited. Mechanisms should be in place to ensure that people have confidential ways of reporting unwanted behaviors without fear of reprisal. Additionally, when such reports are made, they should be dealt with swiftly and fairly.

A Final Word on This Chapter

The views above in no way present an exhaustive commentary on how sex is used and abused. However, they do serve as cautionary depictions of how, when not used in the way God intended, sex can be destructive especially when driven by the need for power and control.

As social and sexual beings, we are driven to seek companionship. How we find this companionship depends on the influence of family, church, and social norms. God gave us sex for our enjoyment. At our best we engage in sexual activity to share intimacy with our significant others, to give life to the next generation, and to meet our basic human needs. At its worst, it lives in the menacing grip of power and control, resulting in the exploitation of the most vulnerable amongst us—women, children, the disabled, the poor, and the dispossessed.

Reflection

1. How do we as a society mediate between the differing views of sex in ways that are life-giving?
2. How can you support youth and children that are at risk of being victims of sexual abuse?
3. How have you been influenced by the commercialization of sex in terms of your spending habits?
4. What can you do to ground your family in a way that they are not succumbing to the unhealthy views of sex?

If you know of a child who is being abused physically or sexually, call your local police.

Finding Your Story in Scripture: Genesis 39–Joseph and Potiphar's Wife

This Biblical text is one of the few if not the only that describes the sexual harassment of a man perpetrated by a woman. In the age of increased awareness and swift responses to sexual assaults, we are reminded that at times men can and do fall victims to sexual violence. Many young men are in need of healing for such abuse but struggle to find safe places to tell their stories. Joseph in some ways exemplifies how power can be used to force to victimize the powerless. As you read Genesis 39 consider your own view of victims and victimizers. How does this story fit in or differ from your views?

Strengthening the Ties that Bind	Helpful Resources
"When reduced to a commodity, sex is used as a means to exploit the innocent and powerless for financial gain and pleasure. As long as sex sells, issues such as sex in advertising, prostitution, and human trafficking will contribute be a blight on the human condition."	National Human Trafficking Hotline 1-888-373-7888 Humantraffickinghotine.org Text 233733 live chat Sex addicts anonymous – SAA 1-800-477-8191 saa-recovery.org RAINN — National Sexual Assault Hotline 1-800-656-HOPE (4673) https://www.rainn.org National Center on Safe and Supportive Learning environments: https://safesupportivelearning.ed.gov/human-trafficking-americas-schools

VI

INFIDELITY:
IF IT HAPPENS, YOUR MARRIAGE CAN SURVIVE

On particularly rough days when I'm sure I can't possibly endure, I like to remind myself that my track record for getting through bad days so far is 100% … and that's pretty good.
—Unknown

Infidelity is an ugly reality all too commonplace in today's world. One would think that we would arm ourselves properly against the very real threat of adultery. Unfortunately, the opposite is often the case; we avoid the subject altogether, choosing instead to ignore it or refuse to entertain the possibility that it would ever happen to us. But affairs do happen. And when they do, they leave in their wake a trail of pain and heartbreak that is nearly impossible to recover from.

In my 16 years of counseling, I have heard all manner of excuses for infidelity. Some deflect blame, claiming the affair was the inevitable result of a flawed partner. "She didn't give me enough (attention/affection/sex)" "If he was more (present/generous/loving)…" Others maintain that forces beyond their control led them to seek extramarital comfort. "I was confused/conflicted about what I wanted. " "I had just lost my job and didn't know where to turn." I could easily list a dozen more.

People who cheat are quickly labeled untrustworthy, amoral, libidinous, or lacking self-control. Our society has little sympathy for the adulterer, and still many marriages and families deal with the fallout of infidelity. An MSNBC survey of 70,000 adults reveals:

- One in five adults currently in monogamous relationships have cheated on their partner.
- More than half of those surveyed said that they have cheated while in a monogamous relationship.
- Married men have the highest rate of infidelity among all groups.
- Couples who are married with children are not immune to infidelity.[17]

There are at least three broad categories affairs can fall into: the sex affair, the love affair, and the emotional affair. We will look at each one in detail, discussing possible causes and suggesting interventions on how couples can avoid affairs before they start.

The Sex Affair

It should come as no surprise that the most common type of affair is the sex affair. The reasons are many and varied. Insecurity, validation, curiosity, or even simply boredom can compel a person to seek out sexual gratification in the arms of another. Men staring down the barrel of middle age often worry about their virility and may want reassurance that they "still have it." A woman approaching middle age may question her attractiveness

---

[17] Jane Weaver, "Many Cheat For a Thrill, More Stay True for Love," NBC News, April 16, 2007, http://www.nbcnews.com/id/17951664/ns/health-sexual_health/t/many-cheat-thrill-more-stay-true-love/#.XCDXxZgrl9d.

and desirability. For her, sex with a different partner can soothe feelings of inadequacy. A sexual affair can be the result of an ill thought out impulse, a reaction to curiosity or boredom. In fact, most sex affairs are just that, folks getting together for the thrill without any commitment to each other. Repeat offenders are often serial cheaters and those battling sex addiction. Still others seek a sexual liaison to escape from reality. The notion that affairs happen because the relationship is in crisis is not always true. Someone may be battling an internal conflict and can't or won't seek the help of a spouse or partner. Individuals with taboo fetishes or unconventional proclivities may be ashamed enough to seek gratification anonymously from a prostitute. Whatever the causes are for sexual affairs, we know that they tend to have devastating impacts on relationships.

The Love Affair

The love affair is typically the most difficult and painful type of affair. It is also the one most likely to produce offspring, last for many years, and be tough to end. Emotions complicate things, and the heart, more often than not, is immune to reason. The lure of sex, while undoubtedly enticing, is nothing compared to the promise of love. For love, people will risk just about anything. The love affair can destroy far more than a marriage; children, extended family, livelihoods, and even the entire trajectory of people's lives can be deleteriously affected. Eventually, the affair will even take its toll on the cheaters themselves as they begin to imagine a new and brighter future, a future that will likely never come to pass. They may discuss ending their current marriages so that they can be together out in the open. Often, the web of deception becomes hopelessly entangled and the lies and betrayals reveal themselves before the tryst's participants are ready, inflicting the worst damage to the greatest number of people including children, extended family members, and friends. The carnage is usually felt for years afterward.

The Emotional Affair

Emotional affairs, while they might not always involve sex, often lead to it. They are affairs of the heart, and breach the boundaries of platonic friendships. There is unrealized sexual tension, inappropriate conversation, and obvious flirtation. These affairs often take place in a professional setting, in online relationships, or amongst friends.

In chapter 4, we looked at the case study of Andy and Jade's failed marriage. Andy's tryst with his assistant, Kate, is a classic example of a person seeking an emotional connection outside of his primary relationship. Feeling isolated from his wife, Andy was able to find someone that was willing to listen to him without judgment. Kate and Andy spent long hours together in the office, eating lunch, working late, and texting. Andy began to rely on her not just to keep his calendar and manage his schedule, but also to meet his emotional needs.

Office relationships can be dangerous, especially between subordinates and their superiors. Andy might not have been able to see the danger because he was used to being in charge. Having sex with his subordinate might have been, for him, a natural progression. Spending long hours on the phone, texting, and talking relentlessly are often indicators that you are crossing the line. Desire can be primal, instinctive, and all consuming. It compels us to seek mates and to procreate. Still, it is important for us to channel our desires and find appropriate outlets to sate them lest they control us. Sex must have its proper place in our lives; there is an appropriate time for it and we should only share it with the person we are supposed to love and trust over all others, our partner. If we don't, sex can destroy hearts and families.

Why Some Survive Affairs and Others Don't

Just because a couple affected by adultery escapes divorce doesn't mean the relationship isn't irrevocably damaged. There can be a number of reasons couples stay together after an affair. One of the primary factors in this decision is children. There are others, though, including:

- The couple believes that marriage is sacred.
- The shame of divorce is too great.
- It would be too financially damaging.
- It is difficult to imagine life without each other (comfort).
- Seeing divorce as a sin.
- They truly love and are committed to each other.

Of course there are those who do decide that divorce is the better option. Again, the reasons for this vary greatly. For some, the affair leaves them shattered and they are no longer able to imagine a future with their spouse. Others view the affair as a symptom of a deeper problem. Possibly the relationship was already strained and the affair sent a clear message that the marriage was over. Some may even use their affair as a door to exit the marriage.

The devastation that an affair brings—including the death of trust and security—can serve as an insurmountable obstacle for some. Trust may be given freely or it may require effort to build. But one thing is unilaterally true. Once damaged, trust requires a mountain of time and effort to restore. And, if destroyed, it's is virtually impossible to get back.

When trust is shattered in a relationship, it sends our mental construct of who we are and what the relationship is into a tailspin. This is so because we define ourselves in the context of our most meaningful relationships. When the things that give us meaning—our profession, our faith, and our family—capsize, we question who we are within those sacred spaces. Simply put, a loss of family can feel like a loss of self. In counseling, I often assess the degree to which a couple is committed to restoring their relationship. The person who cheated may be unwilling to make the changes necessary to save marriage. S/he might find the affair too intoxicating, too fulfilling, or too meaningful to walk away. Unfortunately, there really is little that can be done in these cases. In those instances, I feel a deep sense of sadness for the injured spouse. As an outsider looking in, I must admit the pain for me as a clinician is usually intense, and I can't imagine what it must be like for a wife or a husband to hear that his/her partner is not prepared to give up the affair.

Guarding Against the Affair

When asked what caused an affair, an insightful person will be able to pinpoint the exact movement towards the forbidden. Others throw their hands up in ambiguity. Still others blame the affair on the spouse whom they claim drove them to seek comfort in another. There is a lot that couples can do to safeguard their marriage against affairs. Here are nine basic tips:

1. Remain emotionally connected with your spouse through open communication. This includes sharing vulnerable moments with each other if you feel like you are drifting.
2. Set and maintain proper boundaries with people of the opposite sex. Don't have conversations with a friend in a way that makes you susceptible to crossing boundaries.
3. Maintain an active and consistent sexual diet in your marriage.
4. Keep conversations clean with friends and co-workers. (Col 3:8)
5. Know your weaknesses and pay attention to when they surface.
6. Have a trusted, reliable person like a parent, pastor, counselor, or mentor that you can reach out to for support and guidance. (Pro 11:14)

7. Know when someone is trying to get you into bed. Affairs don't just happen. Sometimes we aren't as wary of people as we should be. Folks will try to pressure you into starting something you are not prepared for. This is not to say that you will necessarily become a victim, but to better safeguard against that potential, know that some people are masters at systematically breaking down your defenses. (Pro 4:23)

8. When we are being wooed, when we feel flattered and noticed, we tend to stop thinking straight. During these times, it is important to consider the consequences to our marriage and remind ourselves what is most important to us.

9. Reach for underlying motives for your behavior. Some people start affairs because:

   - They are bored and need excitement.
   - They are angry and want to get back at their spouse for hurting them.
   - They decide to engage in a counter-affair to get back at their spouse.
   - They are not having enough sex at home.
   - What is new tends to be more attractive and appealing— but the grass is not always greener on the other side.

If you are going to successfully fight the temptation to cheat, it is crucial to ask yourself why you want to be with someone else. For some, the affair has little impact on their conscience. Some people cheat because of their own issues independent of the state of the marriage. Serial cheaters often have some form of sexual addiction which usually has little to do with sexual gratification. This type of addiction is a psychological disorder and something that should be treated seriously including intervention by a trained professional. If you spend most of your day obsessing or figuring out ways to have sex, this should be a red flag.

Reflection

1. Of the major views presented on sex, which are you most drawn to and why?
2. How did you develop such a viewpoint?
3. How has such a view impacted your journey into intimacy?
4. What has been your comfort level engaging your significant other in conversations around the importance of intimacy?
5. As a couple, what might be some anxieties around engaging the conversation about the need for a more healthy dose of sexual activities?

Finding Your Story in Scripture — 2 Samuel 11

Most of us are familiar with the story of David and Bathsheba. The righteous king brought low by lust, thus proving that no one is immune to temptation. There are more lessons to be found in this story if we look closely. David didn't abandon his moral fortitude all of a sudden. No one goes from zero to 60 in sin. His goodness is well chronicled. And, he faced stronger tests than the lure of a naked woman. He successfully resisted killing the man who wanted him dead. So, what made David slip? As you reread 2 Samuel 11, ask yourself the following:

- What was David doing waking up after being home all day? He's a soldier and a king. Shouldn't he be out protecting his kingdom?
- Why did he keep looking at Bathsheba? Why didn't he turn away immediately?
- Why did he keep piling sin upon sin?

Remember, sins aren't just a bunch of disconnected acts. The more we sin the easier it becomes. Can you maybe see a little of yourself in David?

Strengthening the Ties that Bind	Helpful Resources
"The love affair can destroy far more than a marriage; children, extended family, livelihoods, and even the entire trajectory of people's lives can be deleteriously affected. Eventually, the affair will even take its toll on the cheaters themselves as they begin to imagine a new and brighter future, a future that will likely never come to pass."	Affair Recovery: https://www.affairrecovery.com/ "At Affair Recovery, we help people heal from the pain of affairs and betrayal. Our programs are research based, combining a solid curriculum with the strength of collaborative support to provide solace and recovery for both couples and individuals. All of our materials are created by clinical professionals, all of whom have personally experienced infidelity."

VII

AFTER THE AFFAIR: IS IT POSSIBLE TO REBUILD?

If you can watch the things you gave your life to, broken, and stoop and build 'em up with worn-out tools...Yours is the Earth and everything that's in it.
—Kipling

Unfortunately, many marriages fall victim to infidelity. In fact, extramarital affairs are so common in today's culture, we are often resigned to their inevitability. This being true, now more than ever it is important to know that, however painful the betrayal, an affair does not have to mean the death of a marriage. Through hard work, invested couples can rebuild their relationships to be even stronger than they were before the affair. It's true. Many clinicians will tell you that an affair can expose weaknesses within the marriage. Couples should, of course, endeavor to remain faithful to their spouses. Infidelity is not a marriage tool. Still, out of the bad, good can emerge. Chances are, the good was there all along. It just got covered up with the grunge of life. An affair might be the earthquake that forces us to face the weaknesses in our marriage and commit to strengthening them.

There are several key indicators that can gauge whether or not a couple is ready to rebuild. First and foremost, they must be able to maintain some degree of civility. This is a fundamental component of effective communication. If two people remain openly hostile towards each other there is little hope they can heal what's been broken. Second, the person having the affair must be willing to give it up. People tend to want to have their cake and eat it too. This is not possible in a marriage. If the adulterer refuses to end the tryst, s/he must be made to see that there are only two options—end the affair or end the marriage. An unwillingness to break off the affair may be an indicator that the person is too emotionally attached to his/her lover. In this case, the marriage may be unsalvageable.

The decision to cheat is a choice, not an inevitability over which we cannot control. How a person deals with the consequences of an affair once it's been discovered impacts any attempt at rebuilding the damaged marriage. Believe it or not, some continue to proclaim their innocence long after they have been caught cheating. Others, like Andy, cannot bear the weight of guilt and shame and end up confessing their crime to their spouse. Often the guilty party is outed by a family member, friend, or even the lover.

It's impossible to predict how someone will react when a spouse has been unfaithful. Those who were sure they would leave their spouses if they cheated may be the ones who fight the hardest to save the marriage. It's also difficult to gauge how painful the discovery will be. Some will be unable to withstand the hurt of the betrayal and thus be unable to move beyond it. Others more stoic will face the hurt head-on and so can work through it to find healing on the other side. If we are honest with ourselves we will probably find that we are both; at times we are crippled by the pain and at others determined to push through it. It's important to know that it's OK to fall apart. We need to grieve, to allow ourselves to experience the pain as we would any other trauma. Because betrayal is a trauma; it's the death of trust. It's just as important to remember that we are made in the image and likeness of God. He made us strong, able to get back up when we fall. Let's now look at some strategies that can help both spouses stand back up and find the path that leads them back to each other.

The Unfaithful Spouse

If you have been unfaithful, it is up to you to restore the trust which you broke. If you truly want to make your marriage work, you must be completely invested in reestablishing the closeness and harmony you once shared with your spouse. You need to be prepared to put in time, patience, and hard work. Your spouse may make demands that feel unreasonable or disproportionate. They may even be a bit demeaning. Talk to your spouse about it. But remember, s/he is likely feeling insecure and may be trying to get back the equal partnership you once shared. Fair warning, you may have to swallow your pride and find within yourself the humility to give your spouse what s/he needs to feel safe and secure.

Rebuilding your marriage is like running a marathon. You run long and hard without knowing if or when you will reach the finish line. Yet, you keep on running. Some days you feel like quitting and other days you feel like you've made meaningful progress. Some days you feel connected with your partner and others you feel like your efforts have been for nothing. The important thing is to keep running toward the finish line, or in this case toward rebuilding trust.

Reinvesting in your marriage means reinvesting in yourself. When you hurt your spouse, you hurt yourself. For complete restoration, you need to recommit yourself to the marriage, your family, and yourself. If you have children, you need reassure them that you love them and will be their parent no matter what. How do you restore trust? It is an intentional, consistent, and authentic process. Here are some basic rules to follow if you want to repair your marriage:

Stop It!

You can't fix your relationship if you don't end the affair. You must if you want your marriage to work. Remember, you took vows, public ones before God, that you would forsake all others and unite with your wife or husband. I cannot emphasize enough that fundamental to this healing process is to ensure the affair is over. As long as it's alive you will never be able to rebuild your marriage. Don't end the relationship only to go back to it; this will only cause further pain to your husband or wife and will reinforce that you are not only untrustworthy, you are weak. Don't make it your spouse's responsibility to keep you and your lover apart—that is demeaning. It is your responsibility to end what you started.

Turn Towards Your Spouse

This will be a difficult time for your spouse. S/he will experience a range of emotions and behaviors that may not always make sense—angry outbursts, a desire to cling closely to you, or even vacillation from one extreme to the other. One night, s/he might be overly affectionate and another express disgust at your mere touch. These feelings are normal and your spouse is entitled to them. Acknowledge them, respect them, be patient. And, above all, do not invalidate them with expressions of disbelief or exasperation. You are not the wronged party. Instead, be careful with your partner's vulnerability. Show that you are committed to making amends. Be empathetic and attentive, express authentic sorrow, own up to your mistake, apologize. You were the villain, but you can be the hero again. Dig deep to become the person s/he fell in love with.

Respond to Questions

There are varying opinions on how the unfaithful spouse should respond to questions raised by the injured one. Some experts believe that too much information can cause further hurt. Some argue that demanding details about the affair is a violation of privacy. However, others like Janis Abraham Spring believe that the injured party has a right to ask questions like:

- When did the affair start?
- Where did love acts take place?

- Was it purely physical or was it a love affair in the truest sense of the term?
- What drove you into the arms of another?[18]

Those that hold that the unfaithful spouse should respond to any and all questions in detail maintain that it's the quickest way to healing and recovery. I sit midway between the two extremes. It's not so much about how much information you should share as it is about the dynamics of communication and your approach to problem solving. In one case, the injured spouse might be satisfied with moving on as long as you stop the affair and work on restoring trust. In another, the spouse may insist on having all questions answered. Often, the unfaithful person will readily admit to the affair but feel that revealing details is unnecessary. This is most likely the case if the couple has historically struggled with open/clear communication. If your spouse needs more information in order to make some sense of the cause and nature of the affair, then you should share those details. Transparency is a significant part of rebuilding trust.

The Case of Julie and Sam: I Am Afraid to Hurt You Further

The following dialogue between Julie and Sam might help frame the difficult conversation of how much information to share if you find yourself in this situation.

---

[18] Janis A. Spring, and Michael Spring, *After the Affair: Healing the Pain and Trust when a Partner Has Been Unfaithful.* Second Edition, Harper Audio, 2017.

Sam: I have a lot of questions that I will need you to answer because I just don't understand how you could have done this to me, to us.

Julie: I am so sorry that I broke your heart and our vows. I take full responsibility and promise to do everything I can to rebuild the trust you once had in me.

Sam: I need more information about how long you guys have been seeing each other; If you loved him more than you love me; If I did something wrong to make you seek comfort outside of our marriage. Most days I feel like I am going crazy.

Julie: It pains me to know that you even wonder if you did something that caused the affair. The affair is on me not you. This is my doing and I take full responsibility for my actions. Please don't blame yourself. I am ashamed of what I have done to us, it certainly wasn't worth it. Now I'm afraid that I am losing you.

Sam: I feel like I am losing myself in this madness.

Julie: Sam, I want to answer all of your questions as honestly and as truthfully as I can, but I am also afraid that to do so is to hurt you further. I don't want to cause more harm that I have already done. I am so sorry.

Sam: You keep saying that you're sorry, and I know that you are, but I feel like I can't hear your words. Sorry feels so empty. It doesn't ease the pain. I am not asking you to stop saying you are sorry; I just want you to know that I am still hurting even though I know that you regret what you have done. I expected more from you. I always told friends we have struggles, but an affair is something we would never have to worry about.

Julie: Sorry feels empty for me, too. Please tell me what I can do to make you feel better. I too felt that this could never happen to us; I really did. I don't understand how I could have allowed myself to get into that mess. I was vulnerable and stupid.

Sam: I want you to tell me about how the relationship started, tell me what you found attractive about him. Tell me if you had sex with the both of us the same day, did you use protection and should I be concerned about having contracted some form of STI? I need for the both of us to be tested for STIs even if you say you used protection.

Julie: I will answer any and all of your questions starting now, please tell me when you want me to stop or if I am sharing too much. I also think we should try to take a break at least two days out of the week from discussing the affair and focus on other things in our lives. This will give me the opportunity to focus on supporting you and spending time with you. It will also give you a mental break from the pain of what I have caused. Is that OK? I will also make the appointment to see the doctor at the first available time.

In this vignette, Julie's tone is one of empathy and support. She's clearly working hard to repair the breach that she caused in her marriage. Sam's emotions range from self-blame to confusion; Julie attempts to alleviate his pain by paying attention to his need for reassurance and an unambiguous recommitment to their marriage.

Ask for Forgiveness, Don't Demand It

Asking for forgiveness does not mean that you are entitled to it, but it should mean that you are ready to do the right thing. If you are truly sorry, if your request for forgiveness is genuine, you are telling your spouse that you are sorry for breaking your vows, you regret what happened, and you take full responsibility for your actions. In counseling, we teach couples to use "I" statements for effective communication. Asking for forgiveness should include both the use of "I" statements and an authentic apology.

How Not to Say Sorry

> I am sorry, but you pushed me away and he was there, ready and willing to listen to me and meet my needs. I didn't set out to hurt you, but because of your behavior, I felt I had no other choice at the time. For that I am truly sorry.

The above apology is tinged with blame. This individual has clearly decided that she bears no culpability for the affair. The tone is openly combative. It's hard to accept an apology when your defensive shields are up. Further, this apology offers no reassurance of a better future. To put it plainly, this apology isn't healing, it's hurtful.

An authentic apology that's properly crafted can soothe a broken heart. It is important to note that authentic and kind apologies usually don't happen when there is a lot of anger. They are also hard to come by if both persons are looking to leave the marriage. I have been in too many meetings where apologies are mandated. How can an apology be genuine if it's compulsory? An apology that comes as a result of a command is no longer an apology, it is an order followed.

Saying you are sorry doesn't necessarily mean that you will be forgiven in that moment, or even at all. Not only that, but "sorry" does not mean that both individuals are in the same place emotionally. So what does a well-structured apology using "I" statements look like?

I am sorry for cheating on you. I take full responsibility for breaking the trust you placed in me. I am asking for your forgiveness when you are able to. I am also prepared to do whatever it takes to try and make things right.

While expressions of remorse are critical to the restoration of trust, they often sound hollow, meaningless, and woefully inadequate. "I'm sorry" cannot atone for the betrayal of an affair, but, it does lay the groundwork for it. A meaningful apology requires heart and the courage to admit you were wrong. It is the first step to reintegration into community whether within a familial setting, amongst friends, or in a professional context. This may surprise you, but apologizing is not weak. On the contrary, acknowledging your guilt and assuming responsibility for the consequences requires tremendous courage and the wisdom to accept that you're human and, although you've done wrong, you are going to try to do better in the future.

Scriptures tell us, "For with the heart man believeth unto righteousness; and with the mouth confession is made unto salvation" (Rom 10:10). Salvation and redemption are marked by sincerity of the heart on one hand and, on the other, confession. It's not enough to know that we've hurt someone and that we feel remorse. We must also express that remorse explicitly and resolutely to the person we've wronged, vowing to do what it takes to atone.

We can learn a valuable lesson about forgiveness and repentance from Jewish custom. The period between the Jewish High Holy Days Rosh Hashana, the Jewish New Year, and Yom Kippur, the Day of Atonement, invites the community into a time of penitence. During the Ten Days of Repentance, Jewish faithful are called to reflect on their sins by expressing remorse, resolving to avoid them in the future, and confessing them before God. This is a time of deep prayer, fasting, and reflection.

More than that, Jews must endure the tension that stems from the knowledge that, on Yom Kippur, God will render his judgment and seal their fates for the upcoming year. Thus, there is strong motivation to repent and right their wrongs. We all need to experience the kind of humility Yom Kippur requires if we truly wish to mend the wounds caused by our sins.

Resist the Need to Press for Forgiveness

Trying to compel forgiveness is selfish. It's not about what you need. Pressuring your spouse to give something s/he is not yet ready or able to give only causes both of you more hurt. And anyway, being told that you are forgiven does not mean that you are. Forgiveness is not a one-time event. It is a process that happens in increments. It's hard to forgive, remember that the next time you are compelled to push. Society and faith communities alike have misrepresented the nature and anatomy of forgiveness. We cannot strong arm people into forgiving us. Forgiveness more often than not is a destination rather than an event. By that I mean, people forgive when they:

- Can see a safer future than what they have now
- Have worked through and made sense of what has happened to them

- Are able to work through a range of emotions associated with the event including anger, sadness, shock and loss.

Pushing for an apology is more about assuaging your guilt and anxiety than it is about minimizing the suffering of the injured party. Be patient. There will be plenty of time to ask for and be granted forgiveness. At the beginning of the healing process, you should not expect to hear, "I forgive you." It's trite but true: actions speak louder than words. If you work diligently to heal your relationship, forgiveness will come in time.

Share Information

Trust takes a long time to build but can be destroyed in mere minutes. The last thing you need is for new information to surface about your affair. You should work on creating a sense of predictability and transparency in your marriage as a part of your effort to mend it. For example, if your lover attempts to contact you, don't respond. Do, however, tell your spouse about it and discuss with him/her how or if you should respond. Some spouses might not want to be involved and will ask you to deal with the matter yourself. Some ex-lovers can be persistent. Consider changing your number and cutting all ties with your former lover. If it's possible, change your place of employment if that person works with you. Change churches if that person attends the same congregation.

Reinvest in Your Marriage

Focus on your spouse. Make overtures of your love and commitment—large and small: flowers, dinner, dates, making love, conversations about the future, etc. It's your responsibility to prove to your spouse that you will do everything in your power to make the marriage work. Be prepared to respond to your own anger. At some point you might begin to develop an underlying anger and frustration about all sorts of things including:

- The loss of the affair
- Shame and guilt that you have caused your family pain
- Frustration from feeling that your every move is being managed
- Anger from feeling like you are constantly being interrogated
- The isolation that comes with feeling like the villain

These feelings are all normal. If you are aware of them and respond appropriately then you might be well on your way to healing and recovery. It takes courage to reinvest in your marriage, but with grace and time you will surprise yourself at your capacity to grow and change, even during this very difficult period in your life. There's no easy way to recovery. The important thing to remember is that hard doesn't mean impossible. The act of restoring your marriage can also give you the chance to confront some deeply rooted, unmet needs that caused you to step outside of your marriage in the first place. Here is what I know for sure: if your marriage is to heal, you will be the single most important person to facilitate in its recovery. This gives another meaning to the term, "if it's worth having, it's worth fighting for."

Some couples go to therapy to have someone help them manage their recovery. There are times that I do recommend that the unfaithful spouse see a counselor separate from the joint counseling session. I do this because while some things should be worked out together, other issues are endemic. Some of these things might be rooted in your childhood, they may be unresolved trust issues or maladaptive behaviors that have been repeating themselves in many areas of your life, including in your marriage. In these cases marriage counseling would not be appropriate. You need to seek the professional help of someone who will guide you to your own healing so that you might become not just a better spouse, but a better person. Infidelity in this case can serve as the chasm through which light and hope breaks through not just for the marriage but for your personal wholeness and holiness.

The Injured Spouse: Healing is Possible

The discovery that your spouse has been unfaithful is one of the most painful experiences you can have. It can be likened to suffering the death of a loved one. This kind of betrayal is, in many ways, a death—the death of trust, the death of safety, the death of the belief that your marriage was unshakable. In her seminal work *On Death and Dying* (1969), Elizabeth Kubler-Ross presented a linear pathway of the grieving process that one experiences when faced with death—in this case the death of a relationship. Many today will argue that the grieving process is more circular than linear.

Kübler-Ross Grief Cycle[19]

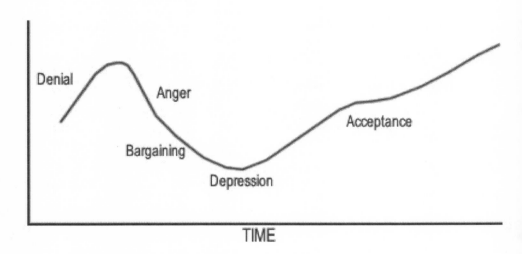

One of the most important things that I can tell you if you are dealing with the pain of infidelity is this: whatever you feel right now is normal. You need not feel guilty about your anger or shame or even the desire to bury the knowledge of the affair so you can go back to your settled world. Your emotions will be all over the place and that is perfectly okay. Later, I will discuss some of the ways that you can take care of yourself during this time.

---

[19] Elizabeth Kübler-Ross, and David Kessler. *On Grief and Grieving: Finding the Meaning of Grief through the Five Stages of Loss,* New York: Simon and Schuster, 2005.

But first let's try to make some sense of emotions that you might feel as a result of the affair.

Denial

It is not unusual for people to respond to the discovery with thoughts:

- Is this real?
- I can't believe it.
- My husband/wife would never do that to me.

During this stage, a numbness usually sets in as the body and psyche try to cushion the impact of the trauma of such a profound loss. Much like what happens with other types of significant loss, the information of the affair will most likely leave you with a surreal feeling. You might feel like you are having an out of body experience or the sense that your life is a movie. Again, the thing to know is that all of this numbness and disbelief is normal. Your body and mind are trying to realign what you thought you had with what actually is. Your confidence might be shaken as your world is upended by an event that will cause you to ask frightening questions about your identity and purpose, not just in the marriage, but in other aspects of your life as well.

As you come to accept what's happened, you will start to replay moments—late night calls, text messages from unknown numbers, changes in schedule, and other secretive behaviors—that you once dismissed. What at the time seemed inconsequential will become glaring evidence that something was happening right under your nose. Don't be too hard on yourself for not seeing it. You are not a fool for trusting your spouse. You would have no reason to assume that a phone call isn't just a phone call, or a late night at work is not just a late night at work. Trust is fundamental in a marriage and a precious gift you bestow on your spouse. The breach of that trust is in no way your fault. Blaming yourself causes undue stress and only re-victimizes you. Remind yourself that the fault does not lie with you, but with your spouse.

Anger

You have a right to be angry; you also have a right to express that anger in an appropriate manner. If you are someone who becomes quiet when you are angry, be quiet in your anger. If you tend to become explosive when angry, lose your temper.[20] Any expression of anger is valid, as long as you are in control of it and not the other way around. You need to manage your anger so that you do not do anything you can't undo.

Bargaining

Kubler-Ross maintains that our response to death comes with a deep desire to bend reality. Those facing death might find themselves praying for second chances at life. They might make promises to do better, to live life with more purpose, or to make amends where necessary. Bargaining in the

---

[20] Violence, however, is never the answer. If you feel yourself losing control to the point where you may become violent, remove yourself from the situation. Step away, cool off, clear your head. Don't re-engage your spouse until you have control over your actions.

case of infidelity includes trying to make sense of what is real and what is not including asking God to make the pain go away. It compels you to question many things about your marriage. Was it wasted time? Was it all a lie? Was the love between you real?

Depression

At some point, shock gives way to anger, anger gives way to bargaining, and bargaining gives way to depression—though these emotions may run concurrently. Depression comes with the realization that you have been tricked, or as one person told me, "I feel like my marriage has been a big lie." Some signs that you might be depressed might include:

- Trouble falling and or staying asleep
- Sleeping for unusually long periods of time
- Change in eating habits such as eating less or over eating
- General anxiety that keeps you in a constant state of panic
- Loss of desire to engage in social and spiritual activities
- Increased susceptibility to illness. Depression and stress compromise the immune system.
- A persistent feeling of not knowing how to carry on

It is critical that during this time, you summon the strength to maintain some routine in your daily life. It's important that you keep getting out of bed, going to work, eating properly, exercising, and spending time with family and friends. To neglect these things might create other crises in your life which can complicate your recovery. Keep to your schedule and routines as much as possible, even when it is difficult and when you feel as though you are just going through the motions. They will reduce your obsession with the affair and may also give you other things to work towards and focus on. As much as you might feel like your world has been capsized, focusing on the parts of your life that are working well will certainly help you to live beyond the trauma of the affair.

Acceptance

This does not mean that you are ok with what has happened. It just means that you have accepted that you have been betrayed. It might also mean that you also accept that this was not your fault. It might also be when you decide that you are not able to continue in a relationship that has brought you so much pain. Acceptance is the starting point for healing.

Surviving Your Dark Days

Ground Yourself in Your Faith

A crisis is likely to cause people to do one of two things. Either they will see it as divine intervention and will thus seek a deeper relationship with God, or they will use it as "proof" that He either does not care or simply doesn't exist and will thus abandon their faith altogether. Those who view the crisis as a sign may turn to prayer and contemplation to help them through their ordeal. While this is the healthier approach, unfortunately, it is not the more common one.

A prevailing notion in today's culture is that if God exists, He would not let bad things happen. Theologians refer to this construct of faith as theodicy. There are three parts to theodicy: a) God is all knowing, b) God is all powerful, c) God is all loving. This theological framework, or our Christian construct of God, has consumed men and women when they fall victims to sicknesses, diseases, disappointments, and betrayal. It is the sense that God has somehow turned away from them. How could a loving and compassionate God allow such brutality and not reveal the reasons why? If He knows what I am going through right now, why do I not feel His presence? If He is all powerful why did He not prevent it? Why did He not offer grace to escape such pain? This sense of abandonment can cause some people to abandon their faith. It is unfortunate, but this is what happens when we practice faith in a very superficial manner.

Take Frequent Breaks

As much as you are tempted to allow the knowledge of the affair to consume you (and it will), it's important to take time away from talking and thinking about. You will have a thousand questions that you will want answered. You will spend many hours trying to make sense of what this means for you both now and in the future. You will have painful decisions to make. These relentless thoughts will overwhelm you if you allow them to run without restraint.

Set Aside Specific Time to Think and Talk about the Affair

As comfortable as denial is, you need time to think and talk about the affair. This requires a tremendous amount of discipline. Here is the truth, if you become too obsessed with trying to figure things out you will drive yourself crazy. You can't control what happened but you do have the power to decide how you want to respond. Allow yourself to cry but don't bury yourself in sorrow. At some point, you will have to get out of bed, open the shades and carry on with your life.

Make Reasonable Demands

Earlier, I noted that the unfaithful spouse will need to acquiesce to your demands. You have a right to ask questions. This does not mean that you will like or even be satisfied with the answers you get. Tell yourself that some things just will not make sense and that many answers will be unsatisfactory. While you are entitled to make demands on your spouse, know that at some point s/he might push back. This, too, is normal, especially if in your pre-affair lives you both struggled with meeting each other's demands. It would be reasonable to ask a spouse to quit his/her job if the lover works for the same company. It might not be reasonable to demand that s/he quit if doing so will send your finances into a tailspin. You might set parameters around avoiding contact with the lover, asking for a transfer to another department when possible, or begin to seek new employment. But to demand that your spouse walk away from a job when it can have devastating consequences on your ability to meet financial obligations would not be in the best interest of the marriage.

Know that You Will Have Good Days and Bad Days

Some days you will feel like you have a new lease on life and are ready to forgive. Other days you will feel tormented. Some days you might go from one extreme to the next. Again, knowing that these are very normal reactions will help you sit with the many mixed emotions that go with being betrayed. The farther away you are from the affair the more good days you will begin to have. The old cliche that time heals all wounds can prove to be (somewhat) true in this case. Take those good days and work on increasing them. Use them to do the things that you like. This is a good time to engage in self-care. Eating healthy and sleeping well cannot be overstated here. Listen to music, go to a movie, see a play, go swimming, do a mini-vacation alone or with others. It's important that you stay healthy physically and mentally. You cannot nurture your heart if your body is not whole.

Get Support

This will continue to be a difficult time for you. You should not have to walk alone. Connect with family members that can support you in whatever decisions you will need to make. Find trusted and wise friends who will be able to give you sound advice. Distance yourself from people who say things like, "if that was me I would..." Sometimes people think they are offering you support but in the end they just make you feel worse, which you certainly don't need during this time. You might want to seek the support of persons who are not as close to you and your spouse. An unbiased opinion can help you to sort out some of your feelings around the affair. A pastoral caregiver can serve in this role, as can a professional counselor, or just a wise acquaintance that you have come to rely on.

Expect to Discover New Information

The decision to begin an affair is a decision to engage in deception, secrecy, and some downright unwise choices. By virtue of such deception, the truth is that the more you learn, the more unanswered questions you'll have. The more you investigate the more unwanted and upsetting truths you will discover. You will have to decide how much you want to know, how deeply you want to dig, and be prepared to live with the consequences of your discovery.

Don't Discount the Good of the Past

As I mentioned, it's not unusual to wonder if the years you spent with your spouse were wasted ones or if s/he ever loved you at all. Don't be surprised if you re-examine each moment of your life together through the lens of doubt. Every gift, every trip, every kind word, every promise made is now insufficient, inadequate, and even disingenuous. Such is the way of a broken heart. I have even seen fathers raise questions as to whether or not their own children were actually theirs. I have seen wives question every innocuous exchange their husbands had with other women. While it might be difficult to not slip into this kind of doubt, you should try to keep a check on this potential downward spiral. Try not to discount the years that you both have invested into the marriage. Remember the good days, the days when you gave thanks for the love that you shared. Consider the things that you created together—children, home, memories. Pain has a way of diminishing or outright discrediting those experiences. Try not to let your hurt and anger erase the past because, in many ways, the past can serve as a roadmap to what might be possible once again.

Healthy relationships are built on trust and covenant. It is through this trust and covenant that we confront life's many circumstances with courage and grace. It's easy for us to unite against a common enemy that might threaten our marriage. When the threat is self-inflicted, it makes recovery more difficult. Additionally, betrayal goes to the heart of how we view ourselves in context of the relationship, our perception of the relationship itself, and what we believe about our world. This is why betrayal is often compared to other significant losses like the death of a loved one. And yet we are all redeemable. As indicated elsewhere, as painful as betrayal and infidelity might be, it doesn't have to spell the end of the relationship. There is plenty of opportunity for couples to face the pain with an eye towards repair, reconciliation, and even fortification against the conditions that led to the betrayal in the first place. Herein lies the tension between the pain of what has been done and what could and should be done moving forward. Those who are able to negotiate their pain and brokenness while undertaking the monumental work of restoration stand a chance of eventually remembering without the sting of the hurt. If they put in the work together, they also stand a chance of telling stories of gratitude and grace. They will tell you that they're glad that they decided to work it out after all.

Reflection

1. How have past relationships affected your perception of love?
2. How has the inability to articulate your needs impacted your intimate space?
3. When betrayed, how do you work through your thoughts and decision-making?
4. If you have betrayed your spouse, have you reflected on the cause for your behavior? How have you taken responsibility for your actions? What have you done to make amends?
5. If you have been betrayed how did you react to the revelation?
6. Consider five things that you can do to engage in self-care during stressful times.

Strengthening the Ties that Bind	Helpful Resources
"The love affair can destroy far more than a marriage; children, extended family, livelihoods, and even the entire trajectory of people's lives can be deleteriously affected. Eventually, the affair will even take its toll on the cheaters themselves as they begin to imagine a new and brighter future, a future that will likely never come to pass."	Affair Recovery: https://www.affairrecovery.com/ "At Affair Recovery, we help people heal from the pain of affairs and betrayal. Our programs are research based, combining a solid curriculum with the strength of collaborative support to provide solace and recovery for both couples and individuals. All of our materials are created by clinical professionals, all of whom have personally experienced infidelity". First Things First: https://firstthings.org/ "First Things First is a non-profit organization that provides healthy relationship skills through classes, events and multimedia outlets. We aim to be a community resource for the Chattanooga area by providing the most up-to-date research, content and educational experiences to all".

VIII

WHAT ABOUT THE CHILDREN:
AFTER THE RELATIONSHIP HAS DIED

It is easier to build strong children than to repair broken men.
—Frederick Douglass

It is hard to imagine that a once thriving relationship can disintegrate into such vitriol and animus. At some point in our lives, all of us will mourn the deaths of relationships whether friendships, work relationships, family connections, or acquaintances. Loss is woven into the tapestry of the human narrative. If we live long enough, we all come face to face with a multiplicity of losses—our youth, our children (as they fly the nest), our health, our loved ones.

The ending of a once loving relationship is one of the most traumatic and painful experiences people endure. This becomes infinitely more complicated when you add children to the mix. In this chapter, we will discuss the challenges associated with ending a relationship when children, especially young children, are involved. We will look at how you can redefine your relationship with your ex in positive ways for the sake of your children and each other.[21]

---

[21] It is worth noting upfront that lawyers, the clergy, and families are often skeptical and suspicious of exes who work well together. They expect there to be hostility and bitterness, not acceptance. The general posture of most is that when relationships end as a

When a marriage ends, so do many other relationships. In-laws become ex in-laws. His friends are no longer hers. Hers no longer his. People choose sides. Lines are drawn. A divorce is not only painful for the couple. It creates a ripple effect of loss felt by many. It's important to remember that your decisions have consequences that affect not only you and your spouse, they impact all those who know and love you both.

It's very possible that while you might want nothing to do with your ex, you still feel a deep connection with his/her parents, family, and friends. How do you navigate those relationships? Do you terminate them as well? Do those choices take a backseat to how you redefine your relationship when children and even pets are involved? If you and your ex share children, you do not have the luxury of cutting all ties. The truth is that children keep people in relationships with each other. This can be mandated by the courts and/or by the heart. Indeed, children are the ties that bind.

It's been the belief that couples should stick it out while the children are still at home. We are told that children need a mother and a father under the same roof no matter how bad things get. Unfortunately, having both parents together in spite of the dysfunction generally does more harm than good. The moral mandate to stay in dysfunctional relationships without

---

result of a betrayal—any type of betrayal—we don't imagine them emerging into healthier interactions.

support has not served anyone well, not served the couple, and certainly not the children.

In fact, the research is clear: some relationships are better off laid to rest for the sake of the children. At a minimum, the decision to stay together should come with significant counseling and marriage support. To mandate that people remain in unhealthy relationships without the necessary support is a moral dilemma. The clergy is particularly guilty of invoking, "What God has joined together let no man put asunder" even when the relationship is toxic. However, some relationships, like those marked by persistent verbal and physical abuse, are worthy of a quick and painless death. And, relationships where pervasive unhappiness persists should be brought to a decisive end or healed for good.

Even though their bond has become threadbare or even broken, many couples are not willing to admit that their relationships are over. Spouses can lead separate lives while living under the same roof. They can even sleep in the same bed even though they have divorced each other emotionally. Many couples stay in loveless marriages because the alternative is either too frightening or they are unable to see their lives any other way. Others may keep up the appearance of togetherness so that they won't have to deal with the shame and ridicule of the community. Still others continue to co-exist for financial reasons.

At the point of divorce, the clergy, lawyers, and family members often support a clean break. We actually find it strange when former couples grow closer after they have split. But what we fail to realize is that by removing the pressure of a conjugal and intimate relationship, former couples may find that they work together better as friends than they did as lovers.

Reasons Why Former Relationships Become Adversarial

Mature couples quickly learn that the divorce is bigger than either of them. Legal systems are designed to pit one person against the other. Lawyers are trained to exploit weaknesses. Pastors are trained to tell people to establish clear boundaries between old and new relationships. Family and friends have their own advice and opinions. Children can get lost in an emotionally draining tug of war. Divorce is never easy; it is not cut and dry nor black and white. To minimize emotional scarring on the children, it's important to remember the following:

- Never bad mouth the other parent. Children become very confused when they hear one parent talk poorly about the other. No one likes to hear bad things about mommy or daddy. Your opinion is yours alone and should not be used to color your child's. When you bad mouth your spouse, you put your child directly in the middle of your fight. This creates a flood of mixed emotions for your child who did nothing to deserve feeling this way. Additionally, such turmoil can be traumatic for children and can thus affect their academic, social, and emotional wellbeing negatively for years, especially when they enter their own intimate spaces.

- Never use children as pawns. It is not uncommon for one parent to refuse the other access to the children out of a misplaced sense of revenge or anger. Your beef is with your spouse, not your child. Children are not material things to be used as leverage. In the end, the person who will suffer the most is your child(ren).

- You don't have to be friends to work together. The notion that you have to be friends with your ex in order to work well together is simply not true. We all have co-workers that we would rather avoid but make the effort to get along with for the sake of the job. So, too, must we develop the skills to work with our exes for the benefit of the children. Admittedly, redefining those relationships is not an easy task, but it is possible.

Marrying Someone with Children

Some people avoid getting involved with folks that have children and exes because those relationships can be complicated. Who wants to see an ex dropping or picking up children from your home, or having children tell you that you can't discipline them because you are not their mother or father? Additionally, having to split financial resources with another family can be frustrating, especially when there are challenges with meeting basic expenses. These are things that cannot be ignored in blended relationships. This is even more complicated in families where there are several children from multiple marriages/relationships.

Making it Work: 10 Co-Parenting Tips

1. Have the conversation about what you imagine your new relationship might look like before the final split. If you wait until after the split, it might be too late.

2. Make sure you keep your relationship struggles and any personal feelings you have about your spouse out of conversations with children. Set clear parameters around your communications with your ex. Your children should be the only focus, other topics are off the table.

3. Set clear boundaries. Your ex is no longer yours; you no longer have the right to his/her life. Avoid asking too many questions. Don't use the children as detectives or informants. You are trying to shield them from the upheaval of your split as much as possible. Don't make them accomplices. This will only confuse and upset them.

4. Use financial resources allocated for the children on nothing but the children.

5. Make a plan for how you will raise your children together without being together yourselves. Stick to it. Make a schedule that divvies up your time spent with your children. Stick to it. This includes not only the big things like holidays and birthdays, but the minutiae such as rides to school, scheduled phone calls, and the like. Having structure can ease the turmoil and uncertainty created by your divorce.

6. Communicate directly with each other. It might feel easier to send and receive messages through your children but this is not fair to them. Whether texting, emailing, or calling each other about the kids, develop a professional relationship that centers around their care and wellbeing.

7. Share information. Both parents should have access to school schedules, doctor's visits, etc. As someone who has spent much time with my children in doctor's offices and at school events, I know that fathers are often marginalized even when we are present. Fathers should make their presence felt in the places their children spend time. Do the routine doctor's visit so that during emergencies you do not appear to be a stranger. Do report card nights and disciplinary conferences so that when other important conversations arise, you are seen as a working partner for your child rather than an imposing figure. Additionally, both parent's names should be on emergency documents and listed as emergency contacts.

It can be incredibly frustrating to be denied access to information about your children whether it be their health, academics, or extracurricular activities. If your child is having trouble in school, both parents should know. If the child needs medical attention of any kind, both parents need to be informed as soon as possible. Any information pertaining to the child, mundane or otherwise, must be made available to both parents. This not only allows both parents to feel equally involved and connected in their children's lives, it can help to alleviate some of the stress of child rearing on the primary caregiver.

8. Let go of the bitterness. You might be angry with your ex for all sorts of reasons, including how the relationship might have ended. At some point, both of you will need to move beyond your anger and hurt. You have to manage your own expectations and nurse your heart back to health for your own wellbeing and the wellbeing of your child. Letting go is easier said than done, but the alternative is not really a viable one. People can become angry when they see their exes giving more and becoming better spouses in new relationships. They begin to wonder why they were not afforded that level of respect and devotion that is being poured into this new relationship. We all learn along the way. It's what life is about, becoming better with time and space. Letting go and forgiving is not a one-time event. It is a process that takes place over time.

9. If you can't come to an agreement on the essentials such as child support and visitation, the courts will do it for you. While I understand that, in many cases, court intervention is unavoidable, I firmly believe that couples should do everything they can to settle things before it gets to this point. The death of an intimate relationship does not have to mean the death of civility. Courts can impose draconian rules that are often not natural to the ebb and flow of life. Also, retaining a lawyer is expensive. You owe it to yourselves and your children to at least try to work things out outside of the courts. But

this, of course, requires trust and compromise which in turn requires humility. It is always in the best interest of the family, whether the parents are together or not, to sort their affairs amicably amongst themselves.

10. Different strokes for different folks. Remember that you and your ex are two distinct persons with different personalities, opinions, parenting styles, and household management structures. The truth is that even people who remain in healthy marriages struggle when it comes to parenting. So it is not uncommon for people who are no longer together but are required to work together for the sake of the children find the task challenging. At the very least you should acknowledge your differences and concede that your approaches to parenting might be different. Open communication is crucial. Take, for example, something as seemingly innocuous as bedtime. 10-year-old Sam might be allowed to go to bed at 11:00 PM when he stays over with Mom, but when he is with Dad bedtime is 8:00 PM. Not only does this inconsistency throw off Sam's circadian rhythm, but it leaves room for him to exploit this difference. Children are good at playing one parent off the other with such retorts as, "but Mommy allows me to stay up as late as I want to" or, "Daddy says that you are too controlling and that it's OK to have candy before bed as long as I brush my teeth." There is no easy way to navigate these differences except through meaningful dialogue. This sometimes means that both parents sit down with their children together and communicate that they are on the same

page and share the same values and expectations for the child's behavior. If this is not made clear, one parent will become the "good" one while the other becomes the "bad."

The Good Parent vs. the Bad Parent

Most children prefer to spend time with parents that make few demands on them. If you only see your child during the weekend, there is a good chance that much of that time will be spent doing something recreational and not on chores or schoolwork. Thus, the weekend parent becomes the "good one." The parent responsible for enforcing discipline during the week becomes the "bad one." Don't give in to that sort of narrative. Be sure to emphasize that your ex is looking out for them by giving them responsibilities. More, you would do well to implement some discipline in your weekend routine. If you don't, evaluate your motive for not holding the child accountable. You might be feeling guilty for not spending enough time with him/her. You might also be experiencing guilt for the disintegration of the marriage. Remember, children need consistency and balance in order to learn responsibility and accountability. The more consistent you both are in this regard, the better it is for your child.

My wife and I are the proud parents of four beautiful children. We have done well in creating a relatively airtight system when it comes to our values and expectations for them. Our three older children—ages 18, 17, and 14—are clear about where we stand on most social and behavioral issues. They are, however, still adolescents and have no compunction about exploiting how well they know us. I have listened in on some intense debates about the differences between Mom and Dad. Dad is the talker and Mom's hand is swift. Dad is less likely to say no to going to friend's house, and Mom is more likely to take us shopping. Our children are experts when it comes to the inner workings of their parents' minds. Generally, children are not given enough credit for the level of knowledge that they possess about their family systems. They strategically submit requests in the absence of the other parent so that they can later say that Mom or Dad said they could. Children are smart and they know how to get what they want. In our marriage, we back each other up on big and small matters. We both tend to fact check:

- Did you ask your Mother?
- What did your Father say when you asked him?
- That's a big request; let me discuss it with your mother and get back to you.
- I'm not sure on that one; why you don't hold off and ask later when we are all together so that you can have our input at once.

When we learn that one of our children tried to exploit a situation by circumventing the instruction of one parent by asking the other, we have a serious conversation with that child about how such deceptive and manipulative behaviors can affect family dynamics and erode trust. We tell him/her that if one of us gave an answer that s/he did not like, they should have done the following:

- Ask the parent that s/he spoke with first if it's OK to approach the other one.
- Negotiate a reasonable alternative.
- We then tell them:
  - You don't have to like the answer you get, but you must accept it.
  - How you respond to "no" is an indicator of your level of maturity. Becoming belligerent and out of order indicates that you need to grow up a bit.

When my wife and I disagree on how to respond to behaviors or requests from our children, we take the conversations "off line." That is, we have those discussions privately. Still, there are times when we allow those disagreements to play out in the presence of the children for a number of reasons:

- The disagreement might be largely insignificant.
- There is a natural and established sense of emotional safety where we can disagree with each other without it getting out of hand.
- Having our kids see how we manage disagreements becomes teachable moments. They can then learn skills of how to listen and present their point without becoming disrespectful and injurious with their words.

- Seeing their parents disagree in a civil manner creates a framework for them to engage each other, friends, and future intimate relationships.

Children today have to contend with many difficulties including being bullied in school, too much homework, extracurricular activities, peer pressure, the list goes on and on. Amid all these struggles, they need mature and sensible parents to help them to navigate the turbulence of growing up in a postmodern world. The quicker parents are able to figure out how to get along for the sake of their children, the better off the entire family will be.

Activity: Areas Where you Work Well Together and Areas that Need Work

In this activity, reflect on major points of contention between you and your ex when it comes to your children and areas where you work well together.

List five areas of interaction where you work well together.

1.
2.
3.
4.
5.

Consider why you think you work well together on these areas. Was it always this way, or did you have to some compromise on how to work through your disagreements?

Now list five topics that you know will cause turbulent emotions.

1.
2.
3.
4.
5.

Why are these topics a trigger for you? How have you contributed to the tension when they arise? If you imagine changing your own thoughts and behavior, what might that look like?

Finding Your Story in Scripture — Wisdom of Solomon (1 Kings 3:16-28)

You all know the story. Two women bring a baby to King Solomon, each claiming to be his mother. Solomon's ingenious solution is to split the infant in two thereby revealing the true mother who, in her horror, quickly relinquishes her claim so that her kid will be spared. Sometimes, custody battles get ugly and those who suffer most are the children. As you reflect on Solomon's judgement and the mother's instinct, think about what you would sacrifice so your child doesn't suffer. I'd be surprised if your answer isn't "everything."

Strengthening the Ties that Bind	Helpful Resources
"It is hard to imagine that a once thriving relationship can disintegrate into such vitriol and animus at the end. At some point in our lives, all of us will mourn the deaths of relationships whether friendships, work relationships, family connections, or acquaintances. Loss is woven into the tapestry of the human narrative. If we live long enough, we all come face to face with a multiplicity of losses—our youth, our children (as they fly the nest), our health, our loved ones."	Marriage Builders: Co- Parenting Tips: https://www.marriagebuilders.com/graphic/mbi5008_qa.html Blended Families Getting Along https://www.youtube.com/watch?v=v8Ffgctm3zQ Focus on The Family: https://www.focusonthefamily.com/

PART II

SIX FAMILY PRACTICES:
LISTENING FOR THE RHYTHMS OF LIFE

In part 2, I invite readers to reflect on some important aspects of family life such as supporting family members during difficult times. This section also deals with the importance of establishing some basic community practices such as playing together and managing the use of technology for the greater good. Consider how you can use these recommendations to strengthen the ties that bind.

IX

RITUALS AND ROUTINES: A CALL TO ORDER

We humans are made for ritual and, in turn, our rituals make us
—John Westerhoff

A few years ago my wife and I went on vacation to the beautiful island of St. Maarten. One morning, we got up at the crack of dawn and went for a walk to watch the sunrise. As we stood on the seawall, we gazed down at the ocean and watched the waves swell and crash on shore, some violent and demanding, others gentle and patient. The rhythm of the ocean, random at the same time completely regular, held us captive as we contemplated the awesome power of God. The systematic chaos of the sea is a good metaphor for our lives. Sometimes they are turbulent and out-of-control, other times they are calm and manageable. We are caught in a perpetual ebbing and flowing. We cannot control the ocean that is our lives, but we can adjust our sails. We endure the back and forth even when it seems to be out of order, because this, in fact, is the natural order of life.

Rituals create a sense of normalcy when trials seek to upend our lives. In his book, *Will Our Children Have Faith?* John Westerhoff argues,

"We humans are made for ritual and, in turn, our rituals make us."[22] When God created the world, he made order out of chaos. Our need for order is built into our DNA. Rituals open us up to a closer communion with the God who framed the universe around order. It's no coincidence that nested inside the word 'spiritual' is the word 'ritual.' We cannot engage in spiritual activities without rituals. They tame the chaos that gets in the way of our relationship with God. For families to thrive there must be order; God demands it. Order helps to:

- Create a sense of predictability;
- Set clear boundaries and expectations for all family members;
- Create a sort of home-base when the world becomes hostile;
- Allow people to function even when some areas of their lives are out of control.

Praxis is the practice of a custom where the theoretical becomes practical. In the upcoming chapters, I will present specific areas of family life that, through intentional rhythmic practices, we can build and preserve lasting family ties. We will deal with:

1. Rituals and routines
2. Mourning and comfort
3. Children's response to loss

---

[22] John H. Westerhoff, III, *Will Our Children Have Faith?*, Church Publishing, Inc., 2012, 53.

4. Creating work-life balance

5. Situating technology in a way that does not impede on your family's wellbeing

6. Embedding leisure as a normal part of family activity

A Call for Rituals and Routines

We are told "success is a do it yourself project." If this is true for family, then we must be intentional about how we move through time and space. Family and marriage are more than institutions; both are journeys filled with adventures, twists, and turns. In today's radical religious environment, traditional rituals and routines are being abandoned in the name of new ways of imagining the Divine. We preach that God is not interested in rituals, routines, or structured religion; what He wants instead is a relationship. This attitude has moved into family life. In the name of progress, we have abandoned many rituals and routines such as eating meals together, participating in corporate worship, having set bedtimes for children, set curfews for teens, how we spend holidays, etc. Having consistent routines and rituals creates a sense of predictability as well as an opportunity for passing on traditions to the next generation.

Those rituals may vary and include things like game nights, morning devotions, or going to a family member's house for Christmas. At the fundamental level, rituals and routines create the space for families to engage in life-giving activities and make lasting memories and serve as a stabilizing force in uncertain times. Furthermore, these spaces help strengthen familial bonds as they allow family members to know one another outside of work, outside of squabbling, and outside of unintentional interactions in the home. All too often, families today, even though they live in the same homes, infrequently see/interact with each other. Complex work schedules, sports and after school activities, and eating in separate spaces make it difficult for family members to have regular meaningful interactions. Strong, stable families are those with closely bonded family members. We need a dramatic change in this trend of living together separately if we want to see an increase in familial stability.

A return to traditional routines and rituals just might be the change we need. These days, the word "tradition" leaves a sour taste in many people's mouths. It is equated with conservatism and a rigid, outdated morality. However, tradition and conservatism are not bad words. In fact, these two words connect our past, present, and future selves.

Routines and rituals create a rhythm that is essential in life. Without them, without a particular way of living or being, our world becomes unstable. Children need rituals to learn moral codes, adults need routines to know how to respond to chaos. Most families have rituals and routines that guide their behaviors and interactions with each other. Some of these are intentional, others automatic responses. When they are, the work of the family and pastoral caregivers is to strengthen the ties that bind. Yet, unintentional routines are often toxic ones. In those instances, families should be encouraged to replace them with healthy, sustaining ones.

We Are All Busy

Isn't it ironic that as our society has become more advanced, the more efficient our means of communication and transportation, the more rigid, less accessible, and more stressed we have become? We are busier than ever before and this isn't likely to change. We are too busy to stay after church for fellowship, too busy to break bread together, too busy to drop in on that neighbor, to visit that elderly family member in the nursing home, to make that phone call to an old friend. The truth is that "I am too busy" will always seem like a legitimate reason not to be fully present, not to build and maintain rituals and routines, not to invest in the people that ought to matter. We stretch ourselves to the point that we become burnt out, sick, and overwhelmed. If we are completely honest with ourselves, many of the things we're doing that we deem important enough to take up every spare moment aren't important enough to warrant sacrificing our faith, our family, and our health.

Start Your Own Tradition

One tradition that I have started in our home is preparing what I call "chuck." I buy a chicken and a duck, debone both, and leave both birds in their original frame. In other words, I remove the skeleton from the birds while leaving the meat/body intact. I then season them with my secret recipe, tie them together, and put them in the fridge for a day or so. On Thanksgiving morning, I then put them in the oven and bake them until they are golden brown. As my family enters our home, it's one of the first things they ask for. Indeed, it is one of the first dishes to be demolished. Both adults and children look forward to eating duck and chicken without bones.

It's never too late to start a new tradition in your family. Traditions are how we pass on our stories to the next generation. While some rituals and routines may seem antiquated, they serve a fundamental purpose; they help preserve our familial identity. Rituals, whether religious, cultural, social, or familial, are critically important to building our worlds. Vacation, religious custom, eating rituals and meal sharing, and holiday traditions are all important to building our families.

Creating a Safe Space for Rituals

Embedded in many spiritual activities is an inherent need for consistent rituals that foster hope through repetitious, life-giving behaviors. Meaningful rituals within all social environments require a deep sense of trust and safety. We can talk all we want about family practices, but if the home is not safe, then it's hard to practice any meaningful spiritual discipline.

Reflection: Rituals and Routines that Matter

In this activity you are invited to think about some rituals you have when it comes to (1) eating, (2) leisure, (3) chores, and (4) faith. You are then invited to imagine other rituals that you think your family could benefit from within those domains. The process of reflection and imagination are important in helping you appreciate and construct deeper ways of living as a family.

Family Rituals and Routines			
Current Eating Rituals	Current Leisure Rituals	Current Chores Routines	Current Religious Rituals
Eating Rituals I hope to start	Leisure Rituals I hope to start	Routine Chores I hope to start	Religious Rituals I hope to start

Finding Your Story in Scripture—Replacing Bad Habits with Good Ones: Col 3:5-17

When you allow the Holy Spirit to guide you, you can develop positive daily routines by replacing bad habits with good ones. If you need some help figuring out which habits are destructive and which should be cultivated, the Apostle Paul gives some sage advice in his letter to the Colossians.

> "And whatever you do, in word or deed, do everything in the name of the Lord Jesus, giving thanks to God the Father through him" (Col 3:17).

X

MOURNING AND COMFORTING:
THESE ARE THE TIES THAT BIND

The world breaks everyone, and afterward, some are strong at the broken places.
—Ernest Hemingway

None of us gets through this life without some pain and suffering. Brokenness can be self-inflicted, triggered by illness or by those who mean us harm, and yes, sometimes by those closest to us. We can endure more than we often realize, especially when we have the support of those we love. Hemingway sagely noted that at some point we all experience brokenness, but what ultimately makes a difference is knowing, in our brokenness, that we are not alone. Not only that, suffering, though unwelcome, can produce serendipitous good. It can bring meaning to life and a deeper appreciation for the time we have on earth, the people in our lives, and the mission for which we are called.

When people don't feel supported during bad times, it is easy for them to believe no one cares. We must make a point to reach out to our loved ones when they have a crisis. If we don't, we risk the relationship we've built with them. So that we don't do this, it's important to understand why we might be disinclined to "step up" and be there for those we care about. Sometimes we fail to be present because the sufferings of others scare us, make us anxious, or overwhelm us. Others' pain can make us uncomfortable, especially if that pain comes with tears, anger, or outbursts. Often, someone's suffering can hit too close to home, reminding us of something in our past we'd rather forget. To escape these feelings, we avoid the hospital visit, the supportive call, the funeral service. Rumi, the 13th century poet, wrote, "That bright fire bird Saladin went like an arrow, and now the bow trembles and sobs, if you know how to weep for human beings, weep for Saladin."

We give so much time to the pursuit of happiness we often don't understand what to make of sorrow. When sadness comes, we latch on to all sorts of untruths:

- I must have done something wrong.
- My family curse is following me.
- God must be punishing me.
- I am undeserving of happiness.
- This is happening because of my past cruelties.

Loss is inevitable. It is not some sort of divine payback; we do not suffer because of ancestral sins. Suffering is part of the human condition—like laughter and joy. The darkness we experience during times of sorrow makes the brightness of the times of joy and laughter that much more radiant. Whether it's the death of a loved one, illness, or losing a job, at some point, loss finds its way into our lives. Sometimes it's not the loss itself but the threat of it that can bring about enormous stress on the family system. Death is one of the most effective teachers, illness is another.

How Do You Say Embryonal Rhabdomyosarcoma?

On a September morning in 2004, our almost three-year old daughter, Vanessa, climbed into our bed as usual. My wife had already left for work. Vanessa began coughing and held her belly in pain. Alarmed, I palpitated her stomach and realized something was very wrong. It was bloated and hard. I immediately took her to the pediatrician. What followed unraveled our world. I was told to take her straight to Westchester Medical Center, that they were expecting us. The doctor called the Maria Fareri Children's Hospital and informed them that he was sending over a child with an enlarged liver. Vanessa was admitted right away.

Tests revealed that our girl had embryonal rhabdomyosarcoma—a soft tissue cancer—in her liver. Her doctors decided they had to move fast. She needed surgery to remove the golf ball sized tumor from her liver. By December 2004 she was hospitalized for days at a time to receive chemotherapy. That Christmas, we packed up our gifts and drove to the hospital to have our celebration there. We did not have control over what was happening to our girl, but we could give her this—giving and receiving gifts and, yes, giving thanks—so that's what we did. Live plants were prohibited so a real tree was out. Instead, we bought a pre-lit, synthetic one, and exchanged our gifts while the twinkling lights made us forget, if just for a little while. It was more than the festive lights and the promise of unopened gifts that gave us respite from our grief and worry. It was the familiar ritual of a Ball Family Christmas that grounded us. It was the reminder of who we were as a family and that we were strong enough to weather this storm. We all need rituals and routines; they give us comfort and strength in times of crises.

For the next year we prayed, we fasted, we wept, we had hope and we despaired, and we did it all together, as a family. We were able to get through those days because we relied on each other. We took turns going to the hospital and the pharmacy, taking her for checkups and staying with her overnight. We worked together not only to get things done, but to keep our family strong. Extended family, my parents, my wife's parents, my siblings, her brother, all surrounded us with their love and support as, together, we focused on getting our baby girl well. Thankfully, 2019 will mark 11 years since Vanessa has triumphed over cancer.

You must be fully present and engaged in times of crisis. It's how you keep your family strong. When she was in 8th grade, our daughter enrolled in a community after-school program that offered extracurricular activities, socialization, life skills, and homework help. The program had a family night where they showcased components of the program. Vanessa was excited about inviting her family to the event. She especially wanted us to bring her 9-month-old sister. No sooner had we arrived when she commandeered her sister, Addison, and disappeared with her to be with her friends. Shortly thereafter, the program director invited my wife and I to see all the amazing work that the students were doing in the program. Students' work included robotics, photography, computer programming, website building, career exploration and assessment, and creative writing, among other things. When we ended up at the creative writing wall, we saw the following piece. Speechless and near tears, my wife and I read these beautiful words:

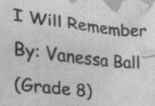

I Will Remember
By: Vanessa Ball
(Grade 8)

When I was two, I had embryo rhabdomyosarcoma – a rare cancer of the liver occurring in infants. Being that I was so young, I really have no memories but, I do remember something. I remember my dad rolling me through the hallways as fast as possible in that environment on my IV pole. And even though my parents were always feeling pain inside, they looked happy. I was happy. I was almost killed but...at the same time I was happy. I think I knew what was going on. I'm pretty positive that I understood that I could've died but somehow I was happy. I remember being bald and not caring and I remember never being left alone. I was never alone because my family was always with me - always there for me. They love me and on some days I feel like I owe them the world because they went so far to keep me healthy. I could never repay them for what they did for me. Its impossible. I can't even wrap my head around the fact.

Thinking about it now, this may just be the single most important experience I've had so far. I think having cancer makes me realize that I have a lot of potential. I mean, I didn't survive for no reason, right? There must be some career path out there for me that I will follow and be successful in. So I survived for a reason and I think someday I'm going to be something great. But, even then I'll never be able to accomplish what they did because no quantity of any material thing I achieve can amount to the love my family has shown me.

I love you guys. I'd be gone without your help and support, so thank you.

Vanessa's original note is rewritten below for clarity and with minor edits.

When I was two, I had embryonal rhabdomyosarcoma – a rare cancer of the liver occurring in infants. Being that I was so young, I really have no memories but I do remember something. I remember my dad rolling me through the hallways as fast as possible in that environment on my IV pole. And even though my parents were always feeling pain inside, they looked happy. I was happy. I was almost killed but...at the same time I was happy. I think I knew what was going on. I'm pretty positive that I understood that I could've died but somehow I was happy. I remember being bald and not caring and I remember never being left alone. I was never alone because my family was always with me – always there for me. They love me and on some days I feel like I owe them the world because they went so far to keep me healthy. I could never repay them for what they did for me. It's impossible. I can't even wrap my head around the fact.

Thinking about it now, this may just be the single most important experience I've had so far. I think having cancer makes me realize that I have a lot of potential. I mean, I didn't survive for no reason, right? There must be some career path out there for me that I will follow and be successful in. So I survived for a reason and I think someday I'm going to be something great. But, even then I'll never be able to accomplish what they did because no quantity of any material thing I achieve can amount to the love my family has shown me.

I love you guys. I'd be gone without your help and support, so thank you.

When I speak of loss, I am not just referring to death. Loss can refer to:

- Losing a job or being unemployment
- Being diagnosed with a serious illness
- Having a mental illness
- Moving away
- Divorce/broken marriage

In *Agents of Hope: A Pastoral Psychology*, Donald Capps talks about the three major threats (despair, apathy, and shame) and the three major allies of hope (trust, patience, and modesty). According to Capps, despair can be understood as, "the perception that what is wanted will not happen, the sense that what is realizable for others is not realizable for me, in spite of the fact that I very much desire it."[23] Despair, apathy, and shame are all associated with loss in one way or another. Our desire is at its peak in the presence of absence, that is, a need unfulfilled or delayed. During these times of loss, we can serve as agents of hope for others. Capps speaks of trust in "reliable others" who can serve as the balm that heals and restores family. It is what Rogers refers to as "unconditional positive regards." That is, every member of the family can be assured

---

[23] Donald Capps, *Agents of Hope: A Pastoral Psychology*, Oregon: Wipf and Stock Publishers, 2001,100.

that, during times of crises, they can rely on the other members for support and comfort.

Mourning is inevitable. Everyone—rich or poor, young or old—will encounter loss at some point. Scriptures are saturated with lamentations, dirges and times of mourning. From the Old Testament to the New, there are many stories where mourning is the key player. In the Gospel of John, we find Jesus at the tomb of Lazarus weeping over the death of his friend. Again, the story of Rachel weeping for her children shakes us to our core as we read, "A voice is heard in Ramah, mourning and great weeping, Rachel weeping for her children and refusing to be comforted, because they are no more" (Jer 31:15). What is not guaranteed during these times is comfort. We must be aware of this and make a conscious effort to combat this darkness by providing light to those who are lost in it. Scripture provides a rich cause for lighting candles for those the darkness has enveloped. 1 Thess 5:5 affirms that we are children of the light who have no dealings with the darkness. We are also called to heed the words of the Apostle Paul in his letter to the Romans: "The night is nearly over; the day is almost here. So let us put aside the deeds of darkness and put on the armor of light" (Rom 13:12).

Most of us find it difficult to see someone in distress. Tears make us uncomfortable. This is why we tend to avoid conversations with those who are mourning. It's not so easy to ignore tears when they come from a family member. Our love compels us to offer comfort and we instinctively reach out to our grieving loved one. But, what happens when the entire family experiences loss? Who provides support and comfort when everyone is feeling pain and sorrow? The case study below might offer insight as to how families respond to grief, how they deal with unexpected and unfortunate change, and how they can support each other. But first, in his book, *Love and Death,* Forrest Church said this about providing comfort, "You don't really have to say much of anything. Just showing up speaks volumes. It takes but very few words to console another - to be with her in her aloneness. 'Can I get anything for you?' . . . 'Can I adjust your pillow?' To comfort another – to bring him your strength – takes more practice, in large part because it requires you to be more comfortable with yourself."[24]

The Ripple Effects of Death

The Case of Elizabeth Mavis Anchor

Mavis Anchor passed away at the age of 67. She was the mother of two children, Mark and Mandy. Mark was married and expecting his first child. Mandy, the older of the two children, was married for 10 years to John but recently got divorced and moved back in to her mother's home with her kids, Sammy and Kate. The divorce was very messy and hard on her and her children. Because she was struggling financially, she and the children moved in with her mother. Mavis, alone in a 4-bedroom house, insisted this was not a burden.

---

[24] F. Forrester Church, *Love & Death: My Journey Through the Valley of the Shadow,* Beacon Press, 2008, 89.

Mandy was happy to move closer to her mother. Her children loved their Grandma and were excited to be living with her. This would be a positive change for them. They struggled with their parents' divorce and missed their father terribly. Mandy told them that their father had a new family and no longer had time to see them. When they talked to Grandma about this, which they did often, she would tell them not to worry, God would work things out. Her words always seemed to soothe their anxieties and fears about the future. She made them feel loved and protected. Because Mandy worked long hours, Grandma woke them, got them off to school, picked them up, did homework with them, and made sure they spent time with Mom before bed. During this period of uncertainty and change, Mavis's support was invaluable.

Two weeks before the children's 8th birthday, Mavis had a heart attack in her sleep and died. The night before she passed, Mavis told Mandy that she was not feeling well. She asked her if she would be able to get off work early. Mandy came home, fed the kids, put them to bed, and made her mother some tea. She asked her if she wanted to go to the hospital but Mavis insisted that she just needed to get some rest. The next morning, before leaving for work, Mandy went to check on her mother and found her unresponsive. She called 911 and within minutes the kids were awakened by emergency personnel going in and out of the house. The neighbors took the kids to shield them from the trauma. Within half an hour, Mark was there with his wife who was 8 months pregnant with their first child. At 6:50 a.m. Mavis Anchor was pronounced dead.

Kate and Sammy knew something bad had happened to their grandmother, but they didn't understand that she was gone and wouldn't be coming back. The divorce had been hard on them, now they lost the most consistent and stable relationship they had. Between trying to make ends meet, working long hours, and dealing with a failed marriage, their mother, Mandy, was often unavailable to the children emotionally, that was where Grandma came in—and now she was gone.

Kate was especially close to her grandmother. When she had difficulties with her friends or had an insensitive teacher, it was Grandma Mavis who intervened, contacting the school and demanding resolution. Kate felt that she could rely on her grandmother to make her troubles go away. Mavis listened to her and built up her confidence by telling her how smart and talented she was. Mavis fostered in Kate a sense of hope, a hope that had now become despair.

Sammy, 5 years younger than Kate, had his own relationship with Grandma. Once she took him alone to the toy store and told him that he could pick any toy that he wanted. Knowing she didn't have a lot of money, Sammy made sure he chose a toy that he felt Grandma could afford. But, what he remembered most was not the toy, it was his grandmother's kindness, something he had not experienced much in his young life. Unfortunately, although Sammy had stopped wetting his bed by the age of 5, after the death of his grandmother two years later he began to do so again. He also became very weepy and listless in school. His teacher reported that he was no longer handing in homework or participating in class. Within one month of his grandmother's passing he had already gotten into several physical fights with other boys.

Mavis's son, Mark, was excited about becoming a father. His mother had been asking him when he would give her grandchildren. He and his wife often went to his mother's home on Sundays for lunch and were excited to bring his soon to be born son with them. Mavis even offered to babysit occasionally when they needed a break. Mark was devastated by the sudden death of his mother. Some nights his wife Jennifer would hear him weeping quietly in the nursery. Unsettled by the muffled sounds that come from across the hall, she didn't know how to comfort him. She decided that if he wanted her to see him cry he would do so in her presence. She nevertheless felt helpless because he chose to mourn privately.

The loss of a grandmother can upend the entire family system. Mothers and grandmothers are often the glue that hold a family together. They help shoulder burdens, provide wisdom during times of chaos, and dispense discipline to children and adults alike. They become invaluable resources and their homes become meeting places for birthday and holiday celebrations, as well as family get-togethers and reunions.

In fact, any change in the family construct can affect the entire system. Death comes to all, and when it does, gaping holes are left both in our hearts and in the fabric of our social and intimate lives. Because this book is also geared to at-risk families, I am proposing that family members turn to each other during difficult times.

So, how might family members offer support to one another while at the same time receive offered support? This is difficult. When speaking to someone whose family is dealing with loss, I often hear, "I am just making sure everyone else is OK; I am fine." If you are that person who is often working to make sure everyone else is OK, then you know exactly what I am talking about.

I imagine a healthy family system where family members both nuclear and extended are able to turn towards each other during tough times. Because everyone is experiencing the same loss, they can share the pain of that loss and, through this, offer comfort to one another amidst the pain. These are the ties that bind. Support in this case is not professionalized; it is not from a third and objective party that is removed from the suffering. There will always be a place for the professional to support families through therapeutic intervention. However, we cannot underestimate the power of words of encouragement, presence, and the warm embrace from another family member who pledges, "we will get through this together."

Reflection

1. What is your general response to seeing another person's suffering?

2. How do you offer comfort?

3. Who are the individuals in your family who are looked to for support during difficult times?

4. How does your family express pain within your home?

Finding Your Story in Scripture — Seeking Comfort in the Psalms

The Psalms can be a great source of comfort during times of sorrow and loss. David wrote many of his songs of prayer while he was persecuted and rejected by his king. They say misery loves company and there's no nobler grief companion than Israel's greatest king. If you're suffering, you might find some solace in David's sorrowful cries to the Lord. Remember, sorrow shared is sorrow halved.

> *Have mercy upon me, O Lord; for I am weak: O Lord, heal me; for my bones are vexed (Ps 6:2).*

> *Hear my prayer, Lord; listen to my cry for mercy. When I am in distress, I call to you, because you answer me (Ps 86:6-7).*

> *The life of mortals is like grass, they flourish like a flower of the field; the wind blows over it and it is gone, and its place remembers it no more (Ps 103:15-16).*

Strengthening the Ties that Bind	Helpful Resources
"The darkness we experience during times of sorrow makes the brightness of the times of joy and laughter that much more radiant."	https://www.opentohope.com/ "Open to Hope is a non-profit with the mission of helping people find hope after loss". Camp Sunshine: https://www.campsunshine.org/ "Founded in 1984, Camp Sunshine provides retreats combining respite, recreation and support, while enabling hope and promoting joy, for children with life-threatening illnesses and their families through the various stages of a child's illness".

XI

CHILDREN'S RESPONSE TO LOSS

I believe that... hope always triumphs over experience. That laughter is the only cure for grief. And I believe that love is stronger than death.
—Robert Fulghum

Our culture has perfected the sterilization of death and all that is included in final arrangements. We bring in professional morticians and funeral directors to manage death for us. We use euphemisms like "passing," "expired," "gone on to be with the Lord," and "not with us anymore." The fear of naming death is the same one that keeps families from dealing with it directly with children and teens. By the time children are five years old we are told that they understand the three components of death: 1) Death is universal, 2) Death is non-functional, and 3) Death is permanent.

We avoid talking to kids about death in part because we ourselves do not have the language or the emotional capacity to express the death of a loved one. Shielding children from the finality of death does not protect them from the anxiety and fear that they already feel. If anything, keeping them in the dark may result in emotional trauma that can plague them for years. Children should not be sheltered from the death of loved ones. Instead, they should:

- Be allowed to see other's grief so they understand they are not alone in their pain;

- Be allowed to express how they are feeling;
- Be able to tell stories of what they will miss about their loved ones;
- Be allowed to participate in funeral arrangements and services where appropriate.[25]
- Consider writing letters to their loved ones;
- Share how the death is affecting their emotions, eating and sleeping patterns, etc. so that they that understand that whatever they feel is normal.

The biggest issue when supporting children during times of loss is knowing how to respond age appropriately and based on the child's capacity to receive the information. For example, telling an 8-year-old that grandma went to heaven is good, but the child should also be told in clear language that she has died. By age 8, all children should have come in contact with death and its core concepts. At this age, most children will have seen dead pets, death in the news, in their faith communities, and in the media. While we know that children understand the core concepts of death, still we shelter them because we don't want them to feel the pain that we ourselves are feeling. The truth, though, is that it's impossible to shield children from death. One way or another death demands acknowledgement by all, both

---

[25] Children are often left out of planning funeral services; but giving them a voice has powerful healing potential.

the young and the old. During times of loss children look to us for answers about how to cope. There are some specific things that we can do to support our children when they are struggling with loss.

Responding to Children's Response to Death

It's normal for us to pull back on some of our activities during times of loss. We have to be careful though, about how we disrupt the routines of children. I have met with many children in school settings who have lost parents, grandparents, and other family members. I try to let them know:

- I am available to talk to them if they need to talk;
- Some days they will miss the loved one more than others;
- They may have many questions that either I or their parents or teachers will try to answer to the best of our ability;
- It's OK for them to play even if they feel sad;
- It's normal to have dreams about the loved one that has died;
- They may become unfocused at school.

How School Can Support Children Dealing with Loss

I have had family members that show up at school to let us know that their family is suffering a loss and that their child's behavior and mood might be volatile. I have also been kept in the dark about a loss or trauma a student has suffered. In instances of the latter, we often find out only when the student experiences a break-down in the classroom. Telling schools what's going on allows school personnel to keep an eye out for the child and respond sensitively to sadness or sudden changes in behavior and attitude. Schools are staffed with social workers, guidance counselors, and psychologists equipped to provide students with needed intervention. As such, families with school aged children should not be afraid to reach out to schools for support. Teachers, too, can support suffering children in their classrooms. Sammy's regressive bed wetting episode while normal, is an important indication that he is not doing well. Taking out his aggression on his fellow schoolmates is another red flag and must be dealt with immediately. If his school is aware of Ms. Anchor's death, they can implement therapeutic support through the counseling department and respond appropriately to his aggression.

Kate, like Sammy, should be given the opportunity to share memories about her relationship with her grandmother. School staff can listen to her concerns such as, "who will support me when things go wrong at school?" They can let both children know that they will be checking in on them on a regular basis. While schools often insist on maintaining rituals and routines for children facing crises and death, they also understand that sometimes children just need a safe space to cry, talk, or engage in some non-academic activities.

Some years ago my wife lost her maternal grandmother as well as her father's only sister. My son felt these losses deeply. He said some things that stunned me—that he was sad about losing people that he loved, that he wished he had spent more time with them. He was mourning missed opportunities to be together with them, laughing and happy.

Mark and Mandy, too, will have to come to grips with the death of their mother. After final arrangements, which can be a very difficult, the family will have to figure out how to restructure their lives without their loved one. I avoid the term "moving on" when counseling someone about how to cope with death. People don't simply "move on" when they lose a loved one. They take the memories of that person with them. They take their pain and despair with them, too. Mark will have to reimagine his Sunday afternoon lunch with his mother and expecting wife. He will have to deal with the fact that his unborn child will never meet or get to know his mother. After the second night of hearing her husband's muffled sobs, Mark's wife went into the nursery and held him as he stood by the window. "Elizabeth Mavis Anchor. We will name the baby Mavis after her." They both wept and then returned to their bedroom, wept some more and then fell asleep in each other's arms—these are the ties that bind.

Mandy, too, will have to figure out how she will manage the children without the support of her mother. As indicated earlier in this chapter, a change in one part of the family is a change to the entire family system. Out of necessity, Mandy may now find her relationship with her brother changing.

Sibling relationships are some of the longest relationships we will have. This makes sense; our parents will most likely die before us. Mandy and Mark can support each other during this time. Mark and his wife moved into the house with Mandy allowing them to pool their resources to soften the impact on his sister. Jennifer, a new mother, is now able to get support and advice from Mandy, an experienced parent. This kind of support can make all the difference in the world. It is the kind of support that is not just imagined during death, but also during other difficult times. With Mandy's permission, Mark met with John, the father of her child, to discuss the impact the loss of Mavis was having on the family. He told John that Mandy will need additional financial support. They spoke about how much the kids miss their father, and that John should consider spending more time with them moving forward.

The conversation, though difficult and heavy, was without animus. John and Mark were friends before John met Mandy. In fact, Mark introduced the two. John expressed how saddened he was about the passing of Mrs. Anchor saying "That lady is a saint; she was beyond kind to me when Mandy and I were married, and even during the messy divorce she never tried to keep me from my kids or fault me for the break-up of the marriage." He thanked Mark for reaching out and said that he felt ashamed of himself for not being there for Mandy, Kate, and Sammy during the most difficult time in their lives. Mark told him it wasn't too late. That evening, once the kids were in bed, Mark, Mandy, John, and Jennifer talked about how best to move forward and support the children and each other. These are the ties that bind after life breaks our hearts. It was Mark Twain who said, "What is joy without sorrow? What is success without failure? What is a win without a loss? What is health without illness? You have to experience each if you are to appreciate the other. There is always going to be suffering. It's how you look at your suffering, how you deal with it, that will define you."

Twain was right, we don't go through this world without suffering. Adults instinctively try to shelter children from suffering, but this is not always possible. The case of Mavis Anchor shows how the loss of one member changes the whole family. But it also shows that death, while most unwelcome, can serve as a catalyst for mending previously broken relationships.

Reflection

1. How has your family invited children into the grieving space?

2. What are your anxieties about how children might respond to death?

3. How might your own childhood experiences with death impact how you shield children from death?

4. Consider how allowing children the opportunity to grieve the loss of loved ones is connected to their own recovery process and how they remember their loved one.

Strengthening the Ties that Bind	Helpful Resources
"The truth is that it's impossible to shield children from death. One way or another death demands acknowledgement by all, both the young and the old. During times of loss children look to us for answers about how to cope."	http://www.scholastic.com/childrenandgrief/ https://www.brookesplace.org/

XII

CREATING WORK-LIFE BALANCE

Teach us to number our days, that we may gain a heart of wisdom.
—Psalm 90:12

We all know you can have too much of a good thing. We need sunlight in order to survive, and yet too much sun can give us skin cancer. We need fats and salt, but too much causes hypertension, heart disease, and obesity. God wants us to find balance in our lives. The creation narrative is very much about balance and order in the universe. Sun rules by day and the moon and stars rule by night. The Garden of Eden is not just a place of paradise, it is symbolic of this balance and order. In the absence of balance, our world becomes undone. In order for life to thrive there must be a balance between plants and animals. Remove one type of bacteria and another goes unchecked. As it is in nature so it is in our lives. We need balance in our families as well. Children need work and discipline but they also need play. Adults, too, must find time for leisure. We are our healthiest when we get a balanced diet of work and play.

God's Insistence on Reestablishing Balance

If the creation narrative is about the ordering of the universe, then the Exodus narrative is about God reestablishing balance after it was thrown out of kilter by Pharaoh. Exodus 5 tells a fascinating tale about the Hebrew people in Egypt trying to strike a balance between labor, leisure, and worship. As slaves, they worked in hazardous conditions. Pharaoh was a ruthless taskmaster. The value of the human person was reduced to that person's ability to produce goods and services. The young were groomed to produce. The aged and disabled, because they had no value as laborers, were considered useless. Aaron and Moses, who served as what we would consider union leaders, approached Pharaoh to advocate for better working conditions. They made what most of us would consider a reasonable request for time off from work. "Thus saith the Lord God of Israel, let my people go, that they may hold a feast unto me in the wilderness." Pharaoh denied the request asserting that he did not know or care about the Lord who requires rest from labor. Instead of rest, he ordered that they be given more work.

Left unchecked, relentless work will always usurp worship, leisure, and rest. Jobs and careers that keep us always on the go will ultimately ruin our play time, prayer time, and rest time. In the creation narrative, God rests on the seventh day. This is a reminder that we, too, must strike a balance between labor and rest. If you feel guilty for taking time off work to take care of personal matters with you and or your family, step back and remind yourself not to allow the spirit of Pharaoh to infiltrate your heart. An employer who threatens you with termination for taking time to care for a sick child or spouse sees you first and foremost as a laborer rather than a person with other primary responsibilities such as the need to attend to family matters. Pay close attention to the mandate, "Thus saith the Lord God of Israel, let my people go, that they may hold a feast unto me in the wilderness."

The preceding chapter dealt with building rituals and routines. But, as with all things in life, there needs to be a balance. Pharaoh's routines were so embedded into the lives of the people that neither he nor the people were able to imagine an alternate way of living. Furthermore, it's worth noting that God wanted His people away from the hustle and the bustle of the daily grind. It's hard to hear God when our every waking moments are spent attending to work even when we are off the clock. Today, companies even give their employees electronic devices to keep them tethered to work 24/7, including during vacation.

You might get paid for working 8 hours each day, but when you've added up the countless hours checking and replying to emails, returning text messages, and meeting tight deadlines, you might find you really work far more than that. When you work constantly, it can be hard to turn off "work mode" when you are at home with your family, doing something recreational with friends, or even lying in bed. If this sounds like you, your life may be woefully out of balance. An honest assessment of how we pass our days may lead us to conclude that Pharaoh is not dead and Egypt has moved into our very lives. These are the ties that bruise.

Before offering some suggestions on how to find balance, we need to look further at root causes for why we construct our work life the way we do. Working to make ends meet is a real struggle most middle and working class families face. It is not unusual for many of us to have more than one job in order to cover our expenses. It is also fair to say that sometimes we work more than we need to because of the anxiety of not having enough, or because we spend more than we need to on things that are not necessary. Sometimes we engage in relentless work because it gives a sense of purpose. And, sometimes we do it to avoid our families. Lately, I have been reflecting on the number of hours I generally work. I have been reimagining what I would do with the hours that I would regain if I should disrupt my current work patterns. I realize that I would spend more time with my family, more time playing, praying and, yes, sleeping. Reflecting on why we work so much can be a dangerous enterprise because the answers might frighten us. It might mean admitting that we prefer to spend time with computers, papers, and other people than we do coming home to a house filled with tension and conflict. Work is important, especially if it advances society and promotes wholeness in our community. It is also important because it gives us the opportunity to have many of our basic needs met. Still, work, like other meaningful human enterprises, possesses a limited good. There are boundaries to work that should be adhered to for our own benefit.

Tips for Creating Work-Life Balance

Here are a few ways to help get you started in maintaining some balance:

Manage Your Time

We are all given 24 hours each day. We can use the minutes efficiently or we can waste them. We all know people that have accomplished impressive feats in short times while others languish in inertia and purposelessness. The Psalmist David's prayer of wisdom is applicable to all of us: "Teach us to number our days aright that we may apply our hearts unto wisdom" (Ps 90:12). Part of that lesson includes: 1) learning to avoid wasting time on trivialities, 2) recognizing that it is impossible to get everything done in a day, and 3) accepting that we have tomorrow to return to work unfinished. Of course, we should avoid rolling over today's work into tomorrow when possible. But, making sure work time doesn't spill over into family time requires you to accept that there will always be more work to be done.

Be Fully Present During Meal Times

Because many families have different schedules, it is not unusual for them to have few, if any, meals together. Between all the extracurricular activities, competing schedules, late night work, and technological distractions, families struggle to manage their time in order to have meals together. Still, sitting at the same table does not always mean that we are fully present with each other. Today, one of the key distractions during family mealtime is the presence of technology. Go to any restaurant on any given night in any city and you will see how technology is silencing important conversations. You are likely to see each family member at the same table buried in an electronic device while being completely oblivious to the other people at the table.

A good time at dinner is more than eating good food. A good meal includes good conversations and reconnecting with each other. Christopher Lasch argues, "As business, politics, and diplomacy grow more savage and warlike, men seek a haven in private life, in personal relations, above all in the family, the last refuge for love and decency. Domestic life however, seems increasingly incapable of providing these comforts."[26] Lasch is asserting that as the world becomes more hostile and less neighborly, people are naturally moving closer to their family system. Because those systems are often fractured and unhealthy, we can become emotionally homeless. Sitting at the same table eating the same food does not constitute communion. To have communion during a meal is to be fully present with each other. It involves passing the plate to the right or the left. It is saying thank you and commenting on the meal. It is a time for memory sharing and wisdom transferring. Consider this, each day family members go off to work and

---

[26] Christopher Lasch, *Haven in a Heartless World: The Family Besieged*. WW Norton & Co., 1995, xix.

school. Both parents work different jobs and children are in different schools having different experiences. By the time most families are under the same roof, night has fallen, homework must be done, showers must be taken, and chores must be completed. This does not leave much time for families to bond and socialize. Thus, mealtimes are important opportunities to share experiences through storytelling to create a common narrative.

The act of storytelling deepens our knowledge of family members and their experiences. Those experiences then become our stories. The dinner table allows family members to share painful experiences, joyful memories, and ordinary stories. Just as importantly, the dinner table is a therapeutic space where empathy is shown, milestones are celebrated, and support is given.

Scriptures are saturated with miraculous stories that occur when people eat together. In John (2:1-12), Jesus turned water into wine. In John (6: 1-14), He took a limited meal and made it unlimited. In both of these stories the driving narrative was scarcity. Not having enough wine at a wedding can leave people grumpy and the hosts embarrassed. Likewise, not having enough food to feed a hungry throng of people can lead to riots. In the end, Jesus was able to turn scarcity into plenty. Eating together is life giving.

Even people on death row are given a last meal. Jesus, whose death was imminent, had a final meal with his disciples. This reminds us that at the end of our journey, breaking bread with those we love is important. Eating together doesn't always mean we're on the same page. Sometimes things might not be going well, but family members should still break bread together. I can't imagine a more appropriate story to capture this than the one found in Matthew 26:

> When evening came, Jesus was reclining at the table with the Twelve. And while they were eating, he said, "Truly I tell you, one of you will betray me."

There is something deeply paradoxical about the text. In it, we find bread and betrayal, the same feet that Jesus would wash would also walk away from him. The intimacy that bought them to the table would also be broken during His time of need. Still, knowing their hearts and the future, Jesus sat and ate with them. Family means living beyond the offenses that might have been done against you.

When we are angry with each other we remove ourselves physically and emotionally, sometimes creating permanent chasms. Keeping set mealtimes pushes families to look beyond their displeasure with each other and move towards forgiveness. Jesus knew that He would be betrayed. He also knew who would deny Him. Still, he sat with them, ate with them, and washed their feet. The danger of isolating ourselves from each other and from the routines that hold us together is that we don't know how well we might recover from such isolation.

Reflection on Eating Together as a Family

- How often do you eat together as a family and are you satisfied with the number of times per week?

- What are some obstacles preventing your family from eating together on a regular basis? How can you reduce those obstacles?

- How does each family member participate in meal preparation? How can you make it more inclusive and equitable?

- What is usually the tone and conversation during mealtime? Is it quiet and conversational? Stressful? Are there practices that involve family members taking turns to share about their day, struggles, and the need for support?

- How much technology is present at the dinner table?

- How do people leave the table at the end of dinner?

- What is the expectation for cleaning up after dinner?

Learn to Say No

If you find yourself saying yes to people at your expense, it's time to evaluate your motives for doing so. The truth is that people will take from you as long as you are prepared to give. They will take your time without reservation and your resources without thinking twice. Learning to say no is an important part of protecting your own wellbeing while setting boundaries for those who need it. Help others if and when you can, but you need not be the sacrificial lamb so that others can look and feel better. If you have the spirit of a martyr, you will continue to give to others without reciprocation. One of my colleagues has a quote on her desk that says "your failure to plan does not constitute an emergency on my part." Folks will squander their time and then ask you to help alleviate mismanagement. I invite you to reflect on the following questions as to why you find it difficult to say no:

1. How has saying yes when asked for help strengthened your relationship with others?
2. What personal benefits can you name that have improved your life by frequently saying yes to the requests of colleagues and friends that ask for your help?
3. By saying yes, are you helping or enabling the other person?
4. Are you perpetuating a cycle of dysfunctional dependency?
5. Are you happy saying yes to others or do you find yourself saying yes begrudgingly?
6. How good are you in asking others for help?
7. What do you think will happen if you should start saying no more frequently?
8. Do you say yes to appease others or remain in their good graces?

Learning to say no is important because it allows you to do your job, get out of work on time, and spend time with family. Early in my college career, I read a short story by Herman Melville called "Bartleby the Scrivener." Bartleby worked in a law firm and at first he did impressive work, but soon the hard working Bartleby's efforts came to a screeching halt. Whatever he was asked to do his response was the same, "I would prefer not to." Of course, I am not advocating this kind of response to work colleagues. Collaboration is needed in order to run any successful business. However, it is important to set boundaries when working with others. Saying no lets colleagues know that you have high expectations of them and that you expect them to pull their own weight. There is nothing so frustrating as seeing a colleague wasting time and resources only to pile work on those who are already working hard. The notion that 20% of the people do 80% the work and 80% of the people do 20% of the work is, in many cases, true.

Avoid Procrastination

During my dissertation work, I vividly remember a meeting with my mentor that left me rather upset. I was dragging my feet on my research and was moving slowly in handing in individual chapters of my project. I had to complete five chapters in total that would amount to about 230 pages of text. In my meeting with him, he said, "Roger, you need to get it done, at the rate that you are going you will not be done until 2017." Never mind that I was pushing to complete my project in time to graduate by the spring of 2015 while working full time and pastoring. I knew then that I had to do better. My mentor said, "I know that you have more on your plate than most of your cohorts, but you said you want to graduate in 2015, so get it done." That was all I needed to hear. I went home, dug in, and kept writing. I wrote while in London on vacation, I wrote while on the train from London to Paris, and then wrote in Paris while my wife was sleeping. We traveled to Florida and to Guyana and to Montreal. It didn't matter where we were traveling to, I packed an extra suitcase full of books, took it with me and wrote every second I got. During holidays and breaks from work I would sit for 10 hours at a time in my dining room and write relentlessly, only getting up to stretch and take bathroom breaks. I would go to bed at 11:00 p.m., get up four hours later and work until 6:00 a.m., shower, wake the kids for school, and head out to work. The process of writing my dissertation taught me a new level of time management. Procrastination, we are told, is the thief of time. Learning the discipline of getting things done on time will free you up to do more with the time that you have on earth. People who are productive tend to sleep less and work more. Of course, I do not advocate not getting sufficient sleep. What I am advocating is that you make the best use of your time to do the things that must be done. One of the reasons I finally decided to buckle down and work hard to complete my dissertation was because I resented the mental burden. I felt like I was thinking about the project every waking hour. I wanted to think about other things. I wanted to imagine writing other pieces, reading books and articles for fun rather than for research. This drove me, and I got it done in a very short time frame. I wanted balance, including more time with my family.

Create a To-Do-List (Daily/Weekly)

Creating an itemized agenda of things that need to be completed in order of priority will allow you to manage your time better. Start your list with things you need to do in a time sensitive manner and, just as importantly, accept the fact that some days you might get through your list and other days you might not. You will feel a sense of accomplishment each time you cross off an item. Not only that, but you will know where to begin the next day. Your list should include when you'd like to do or complete certain items. It should also include the approximate time that you would have completed work in order to get home. If we attempted to quantify the damage relentless work has on our health, spiritual lives, and familial lives, we would be left in deep despair.

Listen to Your Body

Not getting enough sleep will impair your body, mind, and spiritual awareness. Have you ever known people who are always tired? They leave from vacation tired and they return tired. They leave work exhausted and return the next day looking no better. Couples tell me about times when they've been in conversations about important matters when one of them has fallen asleep. When we are tired, we become irritable, irrational, lack focus, and become accident prone. The command to rest is one that we should all take seriously. Rest is a survival mechanism. It keeps us healthy. It is part of our stewardship to being the temple of God.

Leave Work at Work When Possible

The concept of work is always changing. We have moved from being a largely agrarian society to an industrial one to a technologically driven one. With a shift in markets as well as changes in supply and demand along with the use of technology to do work that has historically been done manually, work looks very differently today than it did 100 years ago. In order to remain strong and connected, the modern family needs to be creative with how to juggle chaotic work schedules and quality family time.

Take for example Jane and Peter; Jane is a nurse who works the night shift. She has built much of her life around this shift. Peter works a traditional 9-5 job for a tech company and goes on business trips two to three times a month for four days at a time. With their hectic schedules, they hardly see each other except in passing. They have developed a number of systems to ensure that they remain connected. The chapter on technology will offer some concrete ideas around how to situate balance for our use of technological devices.

Average Hours Worked by Full-Time U.S. Workers, Aged 18+
In a typical week, how many hours do you work?

	Employed full-time
	%
60+ hours	18
50 to 59 hours	21
41 to 49 hours	11
40 hours	42
Less than 40 hours	8

Based on Gallup data from the 2013 and 2014 Work and Education polls, conducted in August of each year

GALLUP

Reflection

1. If you had three additional hours free each day, what would you do with them?

2. How would your stewardship of those additional hours improve your quality of life?

3. Imagine one thing that you can change to give you more time to rest, worship, and play.

Finding Your Story in Scripture—Exodus 5

Exodus 5 deals with the rising tension between Pharaoh and the children of Israel. The people of God requested time off, which in turn angered Pharaoh. Instead of giving them a break from the relentless work, he instructed his supervisors to increase it. This set off a great conflict between God and the Egyptian king. We do not need more evidence than this that God wants us to strike a good balance between work, worship, and leisure. Consider how you can use this chapter to inspire the need to fight for and protect family time from work time and worship time from leisure time.

Strengthening the Ties that Bind	Helpful Resources
"Left unchecked, relentless work will always usurp worship, leisure, and rest. Jobs and careers that keep us always on the go will ultimately ruin our play time, prayer time, and rest time. In the creation narrative, God rests on the seventh day. This is a reminder that we, too, must strike a balance between labor and rest."	Work- Life Balance: https://worklifebalance.com/ Rewire Work – Life Balance https://www.rewireinc.com/work-life-balance http://work-lifebalance.com/

XIII

TECHNOLOGY AND THE FAMILY

So that's the telephone? They ring, and you run.
—Edgar Degas

The Information Age has brought with it a landslide of technology, some good, some not so good—all of it with the potential to both connect us and isolate us. It is unfair to demonize all technology as corruptive and destructive. There is plenty of good that technology has brought to the family structure and society in general. I wrote an entire dissertation over two years from the comfort of my home and on the road. I can count on two hands the number of times I actually went to the university library for my research. I was able to access online just about every document I needed. Technology has brought convenience to our lives in ways that we cannot quantify. Today, we can connect with loved ones near and far through social media, resources such as WhatsApp and Skype, and, of course, cell phones. Social media such as Facebook, Instagram, and Twitter have become common places where people connect with each other, share videos, photographs, memories, and other lighthearted communication. They are where childhood friends and lost relatives are reunited. Technology has brought quite a bit of value to our lives.

Technology, like anything else we use to improve our lives, must have boundaries. Boundaries create both the latitude and the parameters for how, when, and where we use technology within the family system. The internet that allows me to access scholarly research is the same one where criminals can find information on bomb making and websites dedicated to terrorist recruiting can be found. The internet that has hundreds of sites dedicated to recipe sharing and household tips also has a river of salacious and lewd media running through it. Parents and families must be intentional about how to both engage and disengage the use of technology. In this chapter, I will discuss how to limit the use of technology in the family space and how to resist the unhealthy use of technology. First, however, I would like to share a letter New York State Governor Martin Van Buren wrote to President Andrew Jackson in 1829. In it, the governor expresses his concerns that the advent of the railway system will endanger the country's canal system.

Dear President Jackson:

The canal system of this country is being threatened by the spread of a new form of transportation known as 'railroads.' The federal government must preserve the canals for the following reasons:

> *One. If canal boats are supplanted by 'railroads,' serious unemployment will result. Captains, cooks, drivers, hostlers, repairmen and lock tenders will be left without means of livelihood, not to mention the numerous farmers now employed in growing hay for the horses.*

> *Two. Boat builders would suffer and towline, whip and harness makers would be left destitute.*

Three. Canal boats are absolutely essential to the defense of the United States. In the event of the expected trouble with England, the Erie Canal would be the only means by which we could ever move the supplies so vital to waging modern war.

As you may well know, Mr. President, 'railroad' carriages are pulled at the enormous speed of fifteen miles per hour by 'engines' which, in addition to endangering life and limb of passengers, roar and snort their way through the countryside, setting fire to crops, scaring the livestock and frightening women and children.

The Almighty certainly never intended that people should travel at such breakneck speed.

Martin Van Buren
Governor of New York

Today, Van Buren's letter seems almost satirical, but of course the good governor of New York was entirely serious. There will always be people who sound the alarm against change and progress. We need not join those who argue against the use of technology. Instead, what we should do is engage in robust and sensible conversations about how to be intentional about our use of technology so that it does not disrupt the flow of healthy familial engagement, but rather brings us closer to each other and Christ. Thank goodness Governor Van Buren's idea didn't win the day. After all, just consider New York City's complex train and subway system.

Technology as a Disruptive Agent

On a few occasions, our son Michael has demanded that we all turn over our phones to him at the dinner table. After he has collected them, he turns them face down, places them in a far corner of the table, and makes clear that family time should not be interrupted by texting, social media, or phone calls. Of course, his insistence might have been less than altruistic since at the time he did not have a phone himself and felt ignored as everyone else was consumed by the small screen. Technology at the dinner table or during family bonding time can cause us to miss important expressions, conversations, and questions. If technology drives a wedge between family members, it is detrimental to the health and wholeness of the family. If teens or parents are locked away playing video games or watching movies, then that technology becomes the tie that bruises. The irony is that many families are very much in the same space, sometimes inches from each other. But when each is pulled into their own electronic devices they are often worlds apart. It gives new meaning to the phrase "so near and yet so far away." One person might be doing work, another watching Netflix, another catching up on the news, while another is texting, as yet another catching up on the latest adventures of friends on Facebook or Instagram. It is likely that these people are doing two or three of these things at once. Technology was designed to improve lives, but in the end it often isolates us from each other.

Inappropriate Use of Technology

Today, we spend a lot of time talking to people about filtering what they post on social media and what they send to others. Posting and sending sexually explicit images and language is never a good idea. Images posted on social media can be captured and sent to others who can then send it to others. You just don't know where those images will end up, so it's best to avoid sending them at all. Ever so often we see celebrities either suing or being sued for posting a sexual image on social media. It may seem exciting at the time, but it's always a bad idea to capture images of your body parts and send to persons who might one day use them against you. The warning goes out not just to teens, but also to adults who are "sexting" and requesting explicit images of each other. There needs to be a holy reverence to the human body, and yes, some common decency. Today we have all become numb to the pornographic. We can assume that by the age of eight, most children would have already stumbled onto explicit pornographic and violent materials on the web.

The Internet has also become an insidious and sinister tool for predators who:

- Buy and sell child pornographic materials
- Lure unsuspecting children into dangerous situations
- Act out devious and socially unacceptable behaviors
- Hide in plain sight

It has also become the place for people to buy and sell sex. In 2015, news reports broke that the Ashley Madison website was hacked and had all its clients' names published on the web for the world to see. Ashley Madison is a site for those who are married or in a committed relationship who want to connect with strangers for sex. The publication of the client lists ruined many marriages including some notable persons. We are a society driven by the pornographic. Television is ripe with gratuitous sex and violence. Advertisements employ sex, lust, and misogyny to entice potential customers. The proliferation of sex on the web has allowed pornography and misconceptions about healthy, morally acceptable sexual practices to enter intimate and sacred spaces. This obviously can become problematic for several reasons:

- People who love and respect each other and their intimate spaces do not make and sell sex tapes for general consumption
- Pornographic images are not emblematic of healthy sexual relationships
- Sex is often portrayed as something for men and not an intimate experience between two people that care for each other
- Pornography is unethical and diminishes those who buy it, those who sell it, those who produce it, and those who view it.

Too often, I have dealt with teens who made the unwise decision to send images of their breasts and genitalia to others in an effort to be accepted by them only to have those persons share them with others. It's devastating to witness the pain and shame these decisions cause. Parents should talk to their teens about the dangers of sharing illicit images of themselves with others. Never mind the fact that it is a federal crime to transmit sexual images of minors. I teach educators, administrators, and youth workers that under no circumstances are they ever to view those images, even if their intentions are good. The authorities should be contacted immediately if the school has information about such images. If parents attempt to show you, stop them immediately; if staff comes across the images, they must not email, text, or share them—it's a criminal offense that may result in the sender or viewer ending up on the sex offender registry. School administrators have been prosecuted for innocently sharing images with each other. Such images should be safely locked away until they can be turned over to law enforcement.

Pornography is often the elephant in the room that is completely ignored, but the consequences are serious. Pornography is accepted because many view it as an extension of:

- Freedom of expression
- An over sexualized society
- A market driven economy
- An expected rite of passage for the young and the curious
- An essential and normal adult consumption
- A rebellion against the church and what it stands for—holiness

Bullying on the Web: The Ties that Bruise

The story of Tyler Clementi, the Rutgers University student who was in a same-sex relationship and was "outed" by his roommate Dharun Ravi is one example of an extreme case of cyber-bullying. Ravi live-streamed an intimate moment between Tyler and his partner. In the end, Tyler committed suicide after sending out the following final message on social media, "jumping off the GW Bridge sorry." The death of Tyler Clementi sent shockwaves across the country, pushing legislators, primary and secondary schools, and colleges across to institute policies addressing the issue of cyber-bullying. We know that unlike bullying in the physical world, cyber bullies have the opportunity to torment their victims 24 hours a day seven days a week. They also have a wider audience that they can call upon to chime in on the vitriol being spewed against their targets.

Bullying is a real threat to the health and wellbeing of our children. Parents should speak to their children about bullying and being bullied. Families should also hold schools responsible for attending to and monitoring bullying behaviors. The notion that "kids will be kids" and we should therefore accept that peer abuse is a normal part of growing up is antiquated and, frankly, ludicrous. That would be like accepting that domestic violence is normal and merely part of being a family. The research is clear that our children are impacted negatively when they are bullied. Frequent visits to the nurse, problems sleeping, and lack of focus are common among victims of bullying. Children who are bullied tend to underperform in school. They also tend to have symptoms of depression due to the constant fear of being targeted.

Children who consistently engage in bullying behaviors likely have some form of conduct disorder as well as a diminished capacity to feel empathy for others. Furthermore, we know that they tend to continue such behaviors into adulthood. Left unattended, bullying behaviors have consequences on the person engaging in the behavior, the person being targeted, the bystanders, and the overall culture of the institution. Children want to know that we bear witness to their suffering and will protect them. When people are victimized and others see but do nothing, it is one of the worst things they can experience.

We also know that children who are abused or bullied by their siblings and adult family members are more likely to abuse their peers. It is also true the children who have been sexualized and exposed to sexual materials and behavior tend to exhibit inappropriate sexual behaviors towards their peers. These are the ties that bruise. This cycle of abusive relationships continues from generation to generation.

What Children and Teens Can Do If They Are Being Bullied

1. Don't respond to bullying behavior on social media and don't delete any messages received.
2. Seek support from caring adults such as parents, school administrators, pastors, youth leaders, counselors and social workers.

3. Spend time doing things that you like with people that you enjoy being around

4. Remember that you are not alone.

5. Take a break from social media if you are becoming overwhelmed by the rumors and gossip. Sometimes it's best to just remove yourself from the exposure.

6. Block or unfriend that person after you have reported the incident to school officials, Facebook and other sites, parents, and law enforcement.

7. Remember that the bullying says nothing about your character or personhood. People bully because of their own sadistic tendencies, not because something is wrong with you.

Children are bullied for all sorts of reasons: because they are tall, short, smart, special needs, rich, poor, developed, underdeveloped, and the list goes on and on. That's why it's important to tell children that they are created in the "Imago Dei"— in the Image of God. Psalm 139:14 reminds us that we are "fearfully and wonderfully made. Marvelous are your works, and that my soul knows very well." Constant badgering will cause even the bravest of souls to lose their confidence and hope.

What Parents Can Do If Their Child Is Being Bullied

One of the most important things parents should know is that many children suffer in silence. They are convinced that no one will be able to help them so they don't bother speaking up. Honest and open communication with our children can be the very thing that saves them from torment and misery at the hands of a bully. Children can be empowered to act when they know they are not alone. There are many things that parents can do to stop or prevent bullying:

1. Tell your child that s/he is not to blame.
2. Reassure them that you love them and will do all that you can to protect them.
3. Check in regularly with your child about the nature of the bullying behavior whether its physical, verbal, rumors, a cyberattack, or isolation tactics.
4. Reach out to school administrators and teachers about your concerns; hold them accountable. Let them know you fully expect that they will use all their resources to ensure the safety and wellbeing of your child.
5. Pay attention to your child's sleeping and eating patterns, as well as their overall mood and attitude.
6. If you feel the behavior is egregious or that school officials are not responding sufficiently, you need to consider involving law enforcement, especially if it continues.
7. If necessary, take your child to a mental health professional to ensure s/he is not at risk for suicide or depression.

8. If the bullying is coming from another student, you need to have a serious conversation first with your child and then with school officials about transferring to another school.

9. Retain an attorney to communicate the seriousness of the issue.

Sometimes the issue is so complex, toxic, and far reaching, that a change of school might be necessary for the health and wellbeing of your child. A change of environment might be better than keeping a child in a toxic situation. Yet, you need to consider all angles before making a decision this drastic. Over the years I have reminded principals and teachers that in order for us to educate children, we must first create a culture where they feel safe. Our entry point into academia is always through culture. If the culture breeds cruelty and hostility, it will be next to impossible for children to learn complex material. Indeed, if children are afraid to walk to the bathroom out of fear that they will be harassed or beaten, then it becomes pointless to try to teach nouns and pronouns or the Pythagorean theorem. A basic requirement for the learning space is the safety of everyone.

Tyler Clementi jumped off the George Washington Bridge because he felt he couldn't carry on after his private moment was publicly exposed on the internet. People can be cruel, but those who are targets can find strength when good people stand in solidarity with them. You don't have to agree with Tyler's sexual practice to stand with him. You don't have to agree with his decision to keep his sexual orientation private to stand with him. The issue here is that his roommate thought it funny to publicly shame him. Dharun Ravi was prosecuted on charges of invasion of privacy, bias intimidation, tampering with evidence, and witness tampering. Because his cruel actions, on September 22, 2010, a young man with a bright future ended his life. His predator received 30 days behind bars, a $10,000 fine, cyber bullying reeducation, and 300 community service hours. None of this, though, took away the pain felt by Tyler's family and friends.

Technology in the Kids' Bedrooms

It's common knowledge that kids watch too much television—well, streaming media these days. Children with unfettered access to entertainment media can suffer academically, lack focus, have issues with aggression, experiment with sex at a young age, and have disrupted sleep patterns. While there is copious evidence on the impact of television, the internet, social media, and interactive gaming on children and adolescents, we have become numb to it. As a result, many children not only have television sets, but computers/tablets, cell phones, and game systems. In the 90s, we encouraged parents to put the computer in a common space where they could to monitor their children's online activities. They were advised to install parental controls in order to block certain websites. We've since learned to make room for technology. Today most homes have at least one device per bedroom.

These days, teens don't have to secretly order pornographic movies on TV, they can do it for free on the internet. Additionally, because many have their own handheld devices and game systems with internet access, they have access aa plethora of violent games, among other things. When children and teens consume violence and pornography, they get lost in their imagination and psyche blurring the line between reality and fantasy. This is why technology needs to be re-situated in our lives. It's incredible the distance we would go to protect our children, and yet we fail to realize the arsenic that might be present in their hands and in their bedrooms.

As a parent with three teens, I know all too well the task of managing their use of technology. The solution is not to keep them away from it but to 1) educate them on its use, 2) limit their use in time and space, and 3) monitor them so they so don't move beyond the boundaries of your expectations. My wife and I have made the decision to collect all technologies before bedtime. This of course does not work. Sometimes we forget to ask or they conveniently forget to turn them over.

Technology in the Marriage Bedroom

It sounds almost humorous that many people sleep with their phones and iPads in their beds. The bedroom should be a sacred space of confidentiality and vulnerability, a place where couples discuss the day's events and their hopes for tomorrow. It's also a space where difficult conversations are had with apologies made and forgiveness granted. Smart phones, tablets, and other electronic devices have disrupted that space for many of us. As noted before, the small screens have a tendency of sucking us in; they monopolize our focus and, in doing so, erode our interactions with those closest to us. With the advent of Netflix and other streaming media, we can burn through entire seasons of a show without coming up for air. We don't even have to suffer the injustice of advertisements, which, in days gone by, would have at least given us the odd 5 minutes here and there to share a quick word with our significant other. Now, we can, quite literally, be next to each other and yet be gone for hours.

It's a good idea to limit the use of technology in your life. Setting boundaries for yourself will help you establish healthy professional and personal boundaries. Consider the last time that you forgot your smartwatch or smart phone. What did that do to your anxiety level? Social media, text messaging, email, and instant access to news and information have created a level of instant gratification that, when removed, can cause withdrawal symptoms similar to those experienced by drug, alcohol, nicotine, and gambling addicts. Most of us will agree that while technology has made life much more manageable, it's also made it more complicated. Make sure that the technology you use to stay in touch with friends and loved ones does not become a bruising agent in your life. Likewise, be sure that the technology that you use to get work done doesn't negatively impact your mental health because you can't separate work and personal time.

Reflection

1. What would happen if you left technology out of the bedroom? How would you use your time differently?
2. What would you miss about not using your devices in the evening? What would this do to your anxiety level?
3. How would limited technology in the bedroom affect your communication?
4. Do you get up at night to check your phone, respond to email, catch up on the news, or use social media? Does this affect your sex life?
5. How is technology used to mask other issues or avoid conversations?
6. How dissatisfied is your spouse with your use of technology during times that you should be bonding?
7. How do you feel about your own use of technology?
8. How dissatisfied are you with the amount of time your spouse spends on technology?

Further reflection

1. Do you turn off your phone before bed?
2. Have you considered fasting technology? What anxieties would this cause?
3. What are some ways you might reduce how often you: a) check your phone, b) send texts/emails, c) use social media?
4. How might doing the above in number 4 improve your quality of life?

Finding Your Story in Scripture: Samuel 17–David and Goliath, Confronting the Bully

The story of David and Goliath shows us that bullying—the strong preying upon the weak—is no new phenomenon. Where Goliath used physical strength and battle skill to intimidate, today, bullies hide behind technology and anonymity while torturing others online. Consider how you can use this story to encourage young people and adults to fight back (without resorting to anger, counter-bullying, or violence).

Strengthening the Ties that Bind	Helpful Resources
"We should engage in robust and sensible conversations about how to be intentional about our use of technology so that it does not disrupt the flow of healthy familial engagement, but rather brings us closer to each other and Christ."	Stop Bullying: https://www.stopbullying.gov/ "StopBullying.gov provides information from various government agencies on what bullying is, what cyberbullying is, who is at risk, and how you can prevent and respond to bullying". National Youth Violence Prevention Resource Center: https://www.cdc.gov/violenceprevention/youthviolence/index.html "Provides information and links to resources on bullying and violence prevention for parents, teenagers, schools, and after-school programs. Sponsored by the U.S. Centers for Disease Control and Prevention".

XIV

LEISURE: DON'T FORGET TO PLAY

And the city shall be full of boys and girls playing in its streets.
—Zech 8:5

Let's face it, life gets busy. It's nearly impossible to slow down and enjoy it. Our schedules are overflowing and we're always running to or from somewhere important. It's disheartening just how many people do not take a break from the busy noises of their lives. Among industrialized nations, the United States stands out as "the only advanced economy in the world that does not guarantee its workers paid vacation. European countries have established legal rights to at least 20 days of paid vacation per year, with legal requirements of 25 and even 30 or more days in some countries."[27]

Quite the opposite, in the US, employees are rewarded for perfect attendance. If you think about it, this norm devalues human life as it suggests that our worth lies in our devotion to work and nothing else. Those who forfeit vacation time, personal days, and sick days should examine their reasoning for doing so. In the beginning of our marriage, when my wife and I would go on vacation, one of the first things I would do is locate he nearest church so that we could attend service while we were away. After a few

---

[27] Rebecca Ray, Milla Sanes, and John Schmitt. "No-Vacation Nation Revisited." Center for Economic and Policy Research, 2013.

years of this, my wife expressed her concern that we spend an inordinate amount of time working and doing ministry. She reminded me that vacation was meant to rejuvenate us so that we could return to work and ministry energized. The truth is that this took some convincing as I was so used to being in church on a Sunday morning. During those early years, I felt like a fish out of water if I was not in church for Sunday service. With some re-education, my wife and best friend of 21 years helped me to not feel guilty about being on vacation. Rest from our daily drudgeries is important in helping us organize our thoughts, reflect on our progress, and celebrate where we come from. We need to learn how to enjoy what we have worked so hard for.

People on their deathbeds don't typically regret not working longer hours or giving more to their employer. Regret, rather, is borne of time lost to selfish pursuits and disordered priorities—time that could have and should have been spent with friends and family doing the things we love. While it might feel good to be financially successful, it is equally important that we make room for rest and rejuvenation. I had been so programmed for work and ministry that even with a mere five days of vacation, I was compelled to find a church, sometimes driving an hour or more to find one. We would then spend several hours in those services, losing what should have been time spent in each other's company. I had forgotten how to play. Ministry and work became my life rather than just one part of it. Looking back, I can see how my life was out of balance. Now, I eagerly go on vacation to rest and enjoy time with my family. I also find that when I come home, I have a renewed vitality and imagination.

Benefits of Family Vacation

Vacation and leisure should be fundamental and non-negotiable, integral parts of the curriculum of life. They hold untold learning opportunities that should not be underestimated. Those who take vacation only if they have some extra money in the bank think that leisure time is only peripherally important. They'd be wrong. For example, children who are exposed to different cultures and have the opportunity to travel abroad develop a broader and more inclusive view of the world. They make connections between things they are learning in school and their own experiences traveling, interacting with different cultures, and learning about history. Additionally, we know that family vacation makes memories. Part of our responsibility to our family is to create positive memories that are worth recalling and retelling. So many times, we engage others in conversations about their childhood only to hear, "I don't remember much about my childhood because it was just too painful." Others tell riveting stories about the amount of mental and emotional energy that has been spent trying to forget much of their formative experiences. These are the ties that bruise. Family vacations create memories of playing together, appreciating each other, praying together, and reflecting on the eternal favor of God. This is the ties that bind.

Of course, if a family is unstable or dysfunctional, vacations can cause further damage. If there are unresolved issues, vacation can either serve as a bonding opportunity or as tinder on smoldering heaps. Families move about in the same space but often spend little time together. As teens carve out their own lives in sports, after school jobs, and in their own social circles, they have little time left for their families. Adults might have different work schedules and therefore have to plan time to see each other. This is the reality of living in a postmodern world. Families have to fight for time together.

If vacation becomes too much like our day-to-day lives where we tend to encroach upon each other's personal space, tensions can boil over into infighting and hostility. Being "stuck" with each other 24/7 can be overwhelming. Vacation intensifies "pre-existing conditions," if you will. In other words, if our relationships are frayed during our normal daily exchanges, then vacation will exacerbate that fray. If our regular family routines and interactions function relatively well, then vacation can further deepen laughter play, play, and bonds.

If you think that there is a chance that things might fall apart, then as a family you should engage in honest conversations about the purpose of the vacation. You should also agree on what you hope to achieve by the end of your time away together. You might even discuss things that are likely to create problems. For example, my family enjoys eating out; however, I generally become overwhelmed eating out three times a day for 5 or more days in a row. It may sound strange, but I know that at some point I will need a break from sitting down and being waited on. My wife knows that I will want to skip a meal or two and opt to grab something and run. I also know that vacation for her means enjoying as many activities as possible, whereas I need to sleep in a few times. Because we know each other, when planning vacation, we engage in a lot of conversation about food choices, adventures and activities, monuments to visit, downtime, and activities for the kids. We discuss flight options and other smaller details. Because of this thorough communication, we are less likely to fight on vacation.

Five Tips to Vacating Fights during Family Vacation

1. Plan vacation together as a family

Spend time talking about where you want to go. This is a good place to start. While one person might do much of the research about your next vacation, it is important that everyone's voices are heard before final decisions are made. Don't assume that your spouse or the rest of your family will know what you want. If you don't speak up, they might plan things for you that you dislike. When you show disappointment or disdain, it can easily infuriate the planner. Anyone can see how displeasure with the plan when it's too late to change can upset the person who invested time and energy doing all the work. Discussing it beforehand can reduce the chances of this happening. Additionally, planning together can deepen your communication skills and emotional connections as well as create a sense of shared value.

2. Discuss what you hope to get out of the vacation

My wife and I have planned, executed, and participated in many retreats over the years including, marriage, family and leadership retreats. In our planning sessions, we spend hours organizing our thoughts around themes, sub-themes, curricula, team building activities, and speakers. We even huddle together thought-partners that are representative of the various stakeholders and demographics of the retreat attendees. We do this because we understand that we must bring intentionality to what we want to achieve whether in a family vacation or a retreat. Families should say what they would like to do on vacation and why and budget for them.

3. Discuss your vacation budget

How much money you spend on the vacation is important before you start spending those funds. Again, this will reduce the chances of getting into arguments about spending including post-vacation life. You don't want to spend so much on vacation that you don't have enough funds to meet your basic needs once you get home.

4. Decide If Vacation Is the Right Space for that Talk

Sometimes we use vacation as the space to bring up things that are bothering us, or unresolved issues. Be careful with this. Thinking that you have a captive audience to address important and potentially upsetting conversations can backfire. Before having these conversations, the entire family should discuss:

- If you are ok with having such conversations on vacation
- The cost and benefits to having those discussions during vacation time
- How the conversations will enrich your vacation experience
- If there are other times outside vacation time that the conversation can take place
- Will such conversations invoke resentment, tension and emotional distancing?

5. Engage in Shared Interest Activities

Vacation should include new experiences, the familiar, and enriching and memorable adventures. In some families, vacation might include doing things together as well as doing some things separately. For example, while I generally can go without the pool, our kids relish being in the water for hours at a time. Because of this, I know I must be prepared to take them to the beach or pool for extended periods of time. They are also generally patient in waiting for the appropriate time to go to the water. We do this for safety reasons. In our family we do not send our kids off to large bodies of water without being there to supervise and participate in the fun with them; some days are more supervision than fun.

I Don't Have Money for Vacation

If vacation is not a priority then it will be hard to find the funds or the imagination to make the space for it. Contrary to what many think, you don't need a lot of money to have a fantastic vacation. Nor do you need to travel across the country or halfway around the world to enjoy God's creation. With some research, you can find good local deals. Or, within a few hours' drive, most of us can find great attractions and entertainment to make our vacation memorable. Here are some tips for having a vacation on low a low budget:

1. Spend time with friends and family in other parts of the country to eliminate hotel cost.
2. Vacation in a place where you can cook your own meals some days and go out others.
3. Shared rentals, like renting a beach house with friends, can help reduce costs.
4. Search for last minute deals on flights and hotels.
5. Enjoy a picnic and beach in local parks.

Family Play: A Cornerstone of Emotional Connection

Many cultures have convinced themselves that if adults engage children in play, that those children will inappropriately cross the lines of respect and obedience. For this reason, parents often set rigid boundaries with children. The old adage, "if you play with a puppy it will eventually lick your mouth" may serve as one of those ties that bruise rather than bind. Adults and children should engage in appropriate and healthy play for a number of reasons. Playing card games and having game nights, for example, can be another space for families to talk about important issues. It can also be a way of helping children build critical thinking skills, learn teamwork, sportsmanship, and being OK with losing sometimes.

In this chapter, we discussed the importance of carving out time for family vacation whether it be visiting a theme park, throwing a ball in the backyard, or having a picnic in the park. They all lead to the same thing— building ties that bind. I indicated at the start of this chapter that at the end of our life's journey our regrets won't include things like wishing that we had spent more time on the job. We won't wish that we had pleased their bosses more or put in more overtime. Instead, we will wish we had said I love you more, spent more time with our families, laughed more.

One task of a pastor is to preside over funeral services. When constructing these difficult sermons, I frequently remind myself that funerals are for the living and not the dead. And because funerals are for the mourners, I have a responsibility to construct sermons that:

- Capture the life of the deceased through an authentic and dignified biographical storytelling of a life that has come to an earthly end
- Make demands on the listeners to live in accordance with the laws of God so that they might find eternal life beyond the grave at the resurrection according to the Apostle Paul (I Cor 15:50-58) and our Lord Jesus Christ (John 11:25)
- Speak comfort to those whose hearts are broken with grief and pain according to Isaiah (40:1) who said, "Comfort ye, comfort ye my people, saith your God."

I also have the responsibility to remind the listeners to count it a blessing that they are among the mourners and not the mourned. Part of that blessing then requires that they return to their homes with a new sense of purpose. I tell them to laugh until tears of joy leak from their eyes. I tell them to forgive because life is short. Take vacation together. Put on that outfit they've been saving for something special. Wear it now because something special is happening at this very moment. Every minute is special, and the sooner we realize that the fewer regrets we will have at the end of our lives. "Yesterday is gone, sweet Jesus," as the song said, "and tomorrow may never be mine, so help me today to do everything that I have to do." Too many funerals are filled with the expensive flowers that the deceased should have received when they could have enjoyed them, while they were alive. Too many funerals are filled with mourners who only bothered to visit after a loved one has died.

Furthermore, in those sermons I routinely invite the listeners to forgive each other because when we are gone we can neither forgive nor be forgiven. Vacation reminds us not to take ourselves too seriously. It allows us to postpone relentless work, an unending checklist of things to do, and setting alarm clocks to catch the early morning train, beat the Monday morning gridlock or to just get started early on impossible workloads. God desires order in our lives and leisure is one way to bring such order into focus. The writer of Hebrews (4:10) noted, "For he that is entered into his rest, he also hath ceased from his own works, as God did from his." Without a doubt, when we enter into solidarity with such scriptures we learn when and how press the pause button on relentless work. In doing so, our mental health will be the better for it, our relationships will be the better for it, our very work lives will be the better for it, and yes, our spiritual lives will be made richer because we rest as God did on day seven of his creation.

Twenty-five years from now when you look back on your career, the work that you have put in, the promotions received and the tasks accomplished, there is a good chance that you will not say, "oh I wish I had not taken those days off, or, "If I had only completed that project earlier." What you might say, however, is, "I wish I had spent more time with my family." Lost time can never be regained and missed opportunities rarely recoverable. You should be relentless at prioritizing life in such a way that you never short-change your family.

Reflection

1. When was the last time you took a family vacation?
2. What has prevented you in the past (besides money) from taking a family vacation?
3. When you are not well rested, how does it affect the following areas of your life (1) family communication, (2) work productivity, (3) mental acuity, and (4) your sense of creativity?
4. Consider five actions that you will take so as to ensure that you are engaging in leisure as a family.

Finding Your Story in Scripture: Mark 6:30-33

As you read this passage, consider how a busy life can rob you of special moments with families. Jesus made an effort to remove himself and his disciples from the daily grinds of ministry. Even when they got into a boat to find a quiet place, the demands of the ministry were still pressing down on them. The people ran on foot and arrived at the docks before Jesus and his disciples got there. Today, people are able to access us through phone calls, text messages, and social media. They can even tell when you read their messages or when you are active online. It is important that you work on protecting your solitude. At some point, we must all retreat from the hustle and bustle of life to a place of rest and relaxation.

FINAL THOUGHTS

I return to the guiding metaphor and title of this book—*The Ties That Bind and Bruise*. The parable of the prodigal son in Luke 15–the man who demanded that his father give him his portion of the inheritance prematurely, squandered it but was then forced to return home—is the story of a family in crisis. It speaks of a father and sons whose hearts are broken. Yet it is also the story of a father who never stops looking out for his children. It is a story of two sons that had open and honest conversations with their father about their shame and anger. It is a story filled with jealousy, loss, anxiety. It is a story of celebration, forgiveness, and love. This family is no different from ours. At times we are united and at times we are fractured. We bruise each other and we heal each other. We are not perfect, but we are all redeemable. That redemption comes to us and from us with all intentionality. It is my sincere hope that this book will become a resource that individuals, pastors, and counselors can use to find some solutions to current struggles. It is also my hope that the many recommendations, reflections, and insights will help individuals and families chart a better future for themselves. This book offers insight on the power of living more inclusively beyond the nuclear family. It also confronts the harsh reality that families are often times so dysfunctional that we leave each other acculturated to brokenness. It also attends to the fact that many relationships that start out with hope and happiness will crash and burn. Still, we have to pick up the pieces and move on. This includes working together for the benefit of our children.

The second half of the book focuses on developing rituals and routines within our families that are life giving. This includes bringing order to how we live in time and space. Technology within the family is addressed as well as supporting each other during difficult times. The book concludes with playing together. May your life and the lives of your family be blessed beyond measure. And may all of your tomorrows bind you to each other and better days.

Epilogue:

This book is the culmination of 20 years of work as a social worker, pastor, public school administrator, a father and a husband. It was written for a broad audience looking to enrich their familial and professional lives. It is my hope that the stories personal and constructed will help you see your ways through difficult and unending days, and to celebrate the good life has to offer.

BIBLIOGRAPHY

Adler-Baeder, Francesca, Brian Higginbotham, and Leanne Lamke. "Putting Empirical Knowledge to Work: Linking Research and Programming on Marital Quality." *Family Relations* 53, no. 5 (2004): 537-546.

Altman, Richard, and Mervyn D. Kaufman. *The Making of a Musical: Fiddler on the Roof*. New York: Crown Publishers, 1972.

Barks, Coleman, and Mawlānā Ǧalāl ad-Dīn Rūmī. *Rumi: The Book of Love: Poems of Ecstasy and Longing*. New York: HarperCollins, 2003.

Barks, Coleman. *A Year with Rumi*. New York: HarperCollins e-book, 2014.

Block, Peter. Community: The Structure of Belonging. Oakland: Berrett-Koehler, 2008.

Brotherson, Sean E., William C. Duncan. "Rebinding the Ties that Bind." *Family Relations* 53, no. 5 (2004): 459-468.

Brueggemann, Walter. *Sabbath as Resistance: Saying No to the Culture of Now*. Westminster John Knox Press, 2017.

Capps, Donald. *Agents of Hope: A Pastoral Psychology*. Oregon: Wipf & Stock, 2001.

———. *The Depleted Self: Sin in a Narcissistic Age*. Minneapolis: Fortress Press, 1993.

Chapman, Gary. *The Five Languages of Love.* Chicago: Northfield, 1995.

Cherlin, Andrew. "The Deinstitutionalization of the American Marriage." *Journal of Marriage and Family* 66, no. 4 (2004): 848-861.

Church, F. Forrest. *Love & Death: My Journey Through the Valley of the Shadow.* Beacon Press, 2008.

Cloud, Henry, and John Townsend. *Boundaries in Marriage.* Zondervan, 2002.

Denham, Sharon A. "Relationships between Family Rituals, Family Routines, and Health." *Journal of Family Nursing* 9, no. 3 (2003): 305-330.

Doherty, William J. and Jared R. Anderson. "Community Marriage Initiatives." *Family Relations* 53, no. 5 (2004): 425-432.

Dollahite, David., Allan J. Hawkins, and Melissa R. Parr. "Something More: The Meanings of Marriage for Religious Couples in America." *Marriage and Family Review* 48, no. 4 (2012): 339-362.

Dweck, Carol S. *Mindset: The New Psychology of Success.* Random House Digital, Inc., 2008.

Francis, Dauren. *Built to Last: A Successful Marriage and Relationship.* WestBow Press, 2015.

Garbarino, James. *Raising Children in a Socially Toxic Environment.* San Francisco: Jossey-Bass, 1995.

Gates, Henry Louis, Jr. *Finding Oprah's Roots: Finding Your Own.* New York: Crown, 2007.

Gerstel, Naomi. "Rethinking Families and Community: The Color, Class, and Centrality of Extended Kin Ties." *Sociological Forum* 26, no. 1 (2011).

Gottman, John Mordechai, and Nan Silver. *The Seven Principles for Making Marriage Work.* New York: Harmony, 2015.

Green, Richard R. "Cultivating the Wasteland with Technology." In *Television Technology: A Look Toward the 21st Century,* 182-188. White Plains: Society of Motion Picture and Television Engineers, 1987.

Gula, Richard M. *Ethics In Pastoral Ministry.* Paulist Press, 1996.

Hemingway, Ernest. *The Sun Also Rises*. New York: Simon and Schuster, 2002.

Jackson, et al. *The Hobbit: An Unexpected Journey*. Amsterdam: Warner Bros Home Entertainment, 2013.

Kelly, Joan B., and Robert E. Emery. "Children's Adjustment Following Divorce: Risk and Resilience Perspectives." *Family Relations* 52, no. 4 (2003): 352-362.

Klerman Lorraine V. "Multipartnered Fertility: Can It Be Reduced?" *Perspectives on Sexual and Reproductive Health* 39, no. 1 (2007): 56-59.

Kübler-Ross, Elisabeth, and David Kessler. *On Grief and Grieving: Finding the Meaning of Grief Through the Five Stages of Loss*. New York: Simon and Schuster, 2005.

Lasch, Christopher. "The Family as a Haven in a Heartless World." *Salmagundi* 35 (1976): 42-55.

———. Haven in a Heartless World: *The Family Besieged*. WW Norton & Co., 1995.

Laslett, Barbara. "The Family as a Public and Private Institution: An Historical Perspective." *Journal of Marriage and Family* 35, no. 3 (1973): 480-492.

Lerman, Robert I. "Capabilities and Contributions of Unwed Fathers." *The Future of Children* 20, no. 2 (2010): 63-85.

Lichter, Daniel T., and Zhenchao Qian. "Serial Cohabitation and the Marital Life Course." *Journal of Marriage and Family* 70, no. 4 (2008): 861-878.

MacLanahan, Sara and Audrey N. Beck. "Parental Relationships in Fragile Families." *The Future of Children* 20, no. 2 (2010): 17-37.

Masheter, Carol. "Healthy and Unhealthy Friendship and Hostility Between Ex-Spouses." *Journal of Marriage and Family* 59, no. 2 (1997): 463-475.

McGoldrick, Monica, Betty Carter, and Nydia Garcia- Preto. *The Expanded Family Life Cycle: Individual, Family and Social Perspectives*. Harlow: Pearson Education, 2014.

McLanahan, Sara, Ron Haskins, Irwin Garfinkel, Ronald B. Mincy and Elisabeth Donahue. "Strengthening Fragile Families." *The Future of Children* 20, no. 2 (2010): 1-8.

McManus, Michael. *Marriage Savers: Helping Your Friends and Family Stay Married*. Grand Rapids: Zondervan, 1993.

Peyser, Mark. "The Death of Little Elisa." *Newsweek*, December 10, 1995. https://www.newsweek.com/death-little-elisa-180258.

Pilkington, Ed. "Tyler Clementi, Student Outed as Gay on Internet, Jumps to His Death." *The Guardian*, September 30, 2010. https://www.theguardian.com/world/2010/sep/30/tyler-clementi-gay-student-suicide.

Popenoe, David. "A World Without Fathers." *Wilson Quarterly* 20, no. 2 (1996): 12-29.

Ray, Rebecca, Milla Sanes, and John Schmitt. "No-Vacation Nation Revisited." Center for Economic and Policy Research, 2013. http://cepr.net/documents/publications/no-vacation-update-2013-05.pdf.

Sandberg, Cheryl, with Nell Scovell. *Lean In: Women, Work and the Will to Lead*. New York: Alfred A. Knopf, 2017.

Scott, Kieren and Warren, Michael. *Perspectives on Marriage: A Reader*. New York: Oxford University Press, 2007.

Sharp, A. "Two People May Have Committed Suicide After Ashley Madison Hack: Police." *Reuters*, August 24, 2015. https://www.reuters.com/article/us-ashleymadison-cybersecurity/two-people-may-have-committed-suicide-after-ashley-madison-hack-police-idUSKCN0QT1O720150824.

Spring, Dr Janis A., and Michael Spring. *After the Affair: Healing the Pain and Trust When a Partner Has Been Unfaithful.* New York: William Morrow, 2013.

Van Der Kolk, Bessel. *The Body Keeps The Score.* New York: Viking, 2014.

Weaver, Jane. "Many Cheat for a Thrill, More Stay for True Love." NBCNews.com. http://www.nbcnews.com/id/17951664/ns/health-sexual_health/t/many-cheat-thrill-more-stay-true-love/.

Westerhoff III, John H. *Will Our Children Have Faith?* New York: Church Publishing, 2012.

Whitehead, Evelyn Eaton, and James D. Whitehead. *Marrying Well: Possibilities in Christian Marriage Today.* Garden City, NY: Doubleday, 1981.

Wilder, Thornton. *The Bridge of San Luis Rey.* New York: Harper Collins, 2014 (reprint).

Zucker, David J. and Moshe Reiss. "Abraham, Sarah, and Hagar as a Blended Family: Problems, Partings, and Possibilities." *Women in Judaism* 6, no. 2 (2009): 1-18.

Made in the USA
Columbia, SC
09 April 2019